It's hard enough for a writer
just to get published.
But even harder is—**Staying Alive.**

"No one knows the ins and outs of the publishing business better....Spinrad is uniquely qualified to give writers advice on how to make a living in this crazy business....Full of witty and practical information on surviving the hazards of freelancing."

—Stephen Goldin
Author, **The Business of Being a Writer**

"Spinrad, past president of one of the strongest writers' groups, has cast a cold eye over the publishing industry in general, and come up with a book that is not so much a manual for story preparation as an examination of the marketplace and the forces that drive it. A must for the prospective writer, and an enjoyable read for anyone interested in the business of writing and publishing."

—**Publisher's Weekly**

"Analyzes the market from both the writer's and the publisher's viewpoints. His pragmatic advice includes a model writer's contract with step-by-step explanations of each clause. There are also chapters on market forces, awards, and criticism."

—**Library Journal**

STAYING ALIVE

AL♦VE

A▼ Writer's Guide
by Norman Spinrad

The Donning Company/Publishers
Norfolk/Virginia Beach

About the Author:
Norman Spinrad is a past president of the Science Fiction Writers of America. He is a multiple nominee for both the Hugo and Nebula Awards for science fiction achievement. He is also an American Book Award Nominee writer. In addition to a series of stunning novels and collections, including the controversial *Bug Jack Barron, A World Between, The Men in the Jungle, The Star Spangled Future,* and *No Direction Home,* he has written for *Star Trek, Playboy, Omni,* and *The LA Free Press.* He is a tireless campaigner for author rights and is the creator of the "model contract" now in use by several writers' organizations.

Portions of Parts One through Five appeared in somewhat different form in *Locus: The Newspaper of the Science Fiction Field,* and are Copyrighted 1979, 1980, 1981, and 1982 by Locus Publications. Part Six is Copyright 1981 and 1982 by Norman Spinrad.

The Donning Company/Publishers
5659 Virginia Beach Boulevard
Norfolk, Virginia 23502

Library of Congress Cataloging in Publication Data
Spinrad, Norman.
    Staying alive.
        1. Science fiction—Authorship—Addresses, essays, lectures.   I. Title.
PN3377.5.S3S68   1983   808'.02   82-14736
ISBN 0-89865-259-6
Printed in the United States of America

INTRODUCTION
AN EDUCATION IN SCIENCE FICTION

I admit it. I am primarily a writer of science fiction. Which is to say that although I have written and published three "mainstream" novels, a volume's worth and then some of political essays, probably hundreds of film and book reviews, science journalism, political journalism, underground journalism, even a piece on Chinese food, science fiction is central to both my total ouvre and the way I look at things.

It should therefore not be so surprising that this book is like its author. Science fiction is the central subject of *Stayin' Alive*, which after all, was written as a series of columns for a science fiction trade magazine, just as science fiction has been central to my education as a writer. But science fiction, we will come to see, is elusive of definitive description, and includes many events in the non-fictional world. Certainly it includes the question of how writers in general relate to the publishing industry in all its Machiavellian specifics, which, I would contend, is a question of relevance to all persons concerned on both sides.

And that, I think, is what this book turns out to be chiefly about. If I were reviewing this book as a novel, I'd say that the setting of the story is science fiction publishing and culture, and the story itself is about how commerce relates to art along the commercial interface.

Thus, while this is directly a book of pragmatic advice to science fiction writers—or at least the columns started out that way—I think it also turns out to speak to the same questions for writers in general, and, also, perhaps to editors. In a sense, we're

3

all in the same boat, and the science fiction writer's station therein has always been to stand as far up in the bow as possible and try to peer ahead through the mists.

Actually, maybe I shouldn't be so sure that I know what this book fully is, since this project has evolved through all its stages at the instigation of persons other than myself. In a funny kind of way, the columns and this book are products of the very process they seek to elucidate.

About the time I started writing, the Science Fiction Writers of America, Inc. was founded, the organization of which at this writing I am President. In other words, my career and the organization were born together, and I've grown up through it from lowly neophyte to Biggest Cheese. At one point in this evolution, I was Vice President, and I championed the idea that SFWA should fight for a minimum standard contract. I ended up being the principal author of the SFWA Model Paperback Contract for my enthusiasm.

A while later, Stephen Goldin, editor of the SFWA Bulletin, asked me to write a series of clause-by-clause explications. A bit after that, Robert A. Heinlein thought that the Bulletin articles should be published as a pamphlet. So he actually pasted one up with type cut out from the magazine and xeroxed some copies. Which led to the desired effect, namely that SFWA published a neat little pamphlet and distributed it to its members.

One of whom is Charles N. Brown, editor of Locus.

Locus has been described as the "Publisher's Weekly, Wall Street Journal, and Women's Wear Daily" of science fiction publishing. That pretty much says it. Over a fifteen year period under the stewardship of Charlie Brown, it evolved into such from its beginnings as a lowly fanzine.

It was Charlie Brown who got the idea that I should do the column for Locus which has been appearing under the title STAYIN' ALIVE, as an extension of my short course in contract reading for the SFWA. (Which is included in this book courtesy of SFWA, Inc.)

It was Ursula Le Guin, who was using the columns in her fiction course, who suggested that it would be useful, at least to her, to have them collected in a book. And then several editors approached me about the project, including Thomas Hart and Ruth Hapgood of Houghton-Mifflin and Hank Stine of Donning, who finally purchased it for his house.

You begin to see what I mean about this book being a product of the process it tries to describe?

4

This book is not strictly organized in the chronological order in which the columns were written. Subjects of concern, like the book, seemed to want to organize themselves, and so what we have here is a book organized very roughly by subject.

However, since there are people who are into such things, I've numbered and dated the individual columns as they appeared in *Locus*, so that they can be read in chronological order if the heart so desires.

While I've done some minor editing to remove tedious redundancy and summaries of points covered elsewhere in greater detail, I have not allowed myself the wisdom of hindsight. As time went on and market conditions evolved, figures given in one column were revised in a later one; neither were my perceptions graven in the stone of utter consistency. I've left it all in in order to convey a sense of evolution. Only in the section introductions and particularly in the HOW THINGS WORK concluding essay written especially for this book have I tried to put the whole process in some kind of retrospective framework.

Originally, "HOW TO" was the basic thrust of this series of columns and, to some extent, has remained central throughout, though the range of interest this question ended up applied to has evolved and mutated.

So while the scope of the columns broadened and deepened to include matters not entirely circumscribed by the bottom-line imperatives, the economic facts of life were never irrelevant.

Are they ever?

PART ONE
HOW TO

This section basically deals with how to maximize income from books that have already been written and sold, along with a short course in how to deal with American publishers in the form of the annotated "SFWA Model Paperback Contract." Although the annotated contract was written long before the columns in this section, I've placed it at the end because of its technical nature. In addition, I've left in some of the clause-by-clause discussion even when it partially duplicates the material in the other pieces in this section so as to leave the reader with a condensed, rationally organized short-course in contract reading and negotiation for easy reference.

In the light of how the column evolved over time, it is interesting for me to note that by column #6, the column on the problems of non-Anglophone sf writers, I was already beginning to allow questions of morality to creep into the discourse on economic matters by the back door, and I was already beginning to address some suggestions to editors and publishers as well as writers.

Which only goes to show that you can't get very far into a discussion ,of economic survival as a writer without rather quickly coming up against both issues of justice and the internal economics of the publishing industry itself. And as you penetrate deeper and deeper into the sf genre, where the same person may be writer, editor, critic, and even publisher, the distinctions begin to blur even more, and a certain sense of community begins to emerge. A sense of community which either never quite existed in

9

the larger literary world, or which seems to have been all but snuffed out by economic self-interest. SFWA, for example, is the only writer's organization I know of which simultaneously functions as a quasi-union on the barricades and as a sort of trade association of the genre in relation to the public at large, allowing membership on an affiliate basis to editors, publishers, and critics as well as writers.

Which, of course, is not to say that economic self-interest and pecuniary hardball playing don't go on all the time!

AUGUST 1979
COLUMN 1

This is going to be a column about surviving as a science fiction writer (and ideally on caviar and champagne rather than Big Macs and Ripple).

A word about my qualifications and where I'm coming from. I am a two-time Vice President and President of SFWA and former Chairman of the Grievance Committee, and at the beginning of my career, I was a sub-agent at Scott Meredith, 1965-1966. More to the point, perhaps, that was the *last* non-writing job I was forced to endure. I have survived entirely as a writer since 1966—without any one huge-selling book, without non-writing income, without writing anything I had to take my name off, without doing all that much television, and basically without writing anything I didn't really want to write. During this time, I have published eight science fiction novels, three collections of short stories, two anthologies, one collection of essays, two mainstream novels, about 50 short stories, and a whole shitload of articles, film reviews, etc. Also about half a dozen assorted scripts and/or TV formats.

The point of any recitation of my credits being not so much my masterly authority as to establish the fact that I haven't been making it on volume. It takes me about half a year to write the average novel, plus another few months to bring it from inspiration to page one of the first draft, plus half a year afterward before I'm usually ready to tackle a novel again. And until fairly recently, I wasn't getting large advances either.

How then do I do it? What's the secret?

There is no one Big Secret. But there sure are a lot of little ones. And if there is one Big Secret, it is just that—taking advantage of all the little ones.

Secret Number One: a book doesn't make any money for you

if it's out of print.

There is—or should be—a reversion clause in every book contract. Basically this says that if your book is out of print after three or five years (depending upon the contract), you write a registered letter to the publisher demanding that they put it back into print within six months. If they do so, it's out there earning royalties for you. And if they don't, the book reverts to you in six months, and you can sell it elsewhere.

Never sign a contract without a reversion clause. Always keep the reversion date in the back of your mind and write your reversion letters promptly. Most mainstream best-sellers are out of print, dead, and forgotten in five years, but science fiction novels *stay in print* if the author works at it. My current agent, Jane Rotrosen, doesn't handle much science fiction, and was mighty dubious about the worth of reverting two old books and trying to sell them. The two books were *Bug Jack Barron* and *The Iron Dream,* and the original advances totalled $7,000. Somewhat to her surprise, Jane was able to resell them for $20,000. She is now a believer in reverting and reselling science fiction novels.

As a matter of fact, with the exception of *The Men in the Jungle,* on which I signed a bad Doubleday contract without a reversion clause, I've reverted and resold all my out of print sf novels at least once (and Doubleday reverted the paperback rights on *Men in the Jungle* and resold them). Aside from the aforementioned resales of *Bug Jack Barron* and *The Iron Dream,* I reverted *The Solarians* from Paperback Library (original advance $1,250), resold it to Belmont for $1,000, collected another $1,000 in royalties, reverted it again, and am now waiting for the right buyer; I reverted *Agent of Chaos* (original advance $1,500) and resold it to Popular Library for $3,000.

In other words, on four books, the total original advances for which came to $9,750, I have thusfar made a total of $28,500 in resales! We are not talkig about peanuts here. We are talking about not having to write twenty-eight porn novels, or twenty Laser quickies for Roger Elwood, or four or five screenplay novelizations, or 2,850,000 words for *Amazing* at 1¢ per, folks! We are talking about the equation between money and artistic freedom, and we are proving that virtue can be its own reward in dollars and cents.

Of course there are a couple of catches here, the first of which has little to do with virtue at all. Far from it. You see, in order to revert your book, you must prove to the publisher's own satisfaction that it is out of print. Which in reality means catching them in some admission that the book is out of print, since they're not about to tell you, Charley.

In the good old days, a royalty statement gave you figures for print run, sales, and returns. When sales and returns equalled print run, the book was QED out of print, and not the slickest shyster in the world could claim otherwise.

Now, however, royalty statements are about as straightforward as a professional writer's income tax return, and "out of print" can rarely be proven from internal evidence. You needs be as tricky as they are sometimes. For instance, get ahold of a copy of the monthly order form the publisher sends to book stores. If your book ain't on it, it's not being offered for sale, is it, which means it is legally out of print by their own updated definition. Or have a cooperative book seller order it for you. If he gets back a letter of regret to the effect that the book isn't available, there's a magic piece of paper too.

When all else fails, and if you're dealing with a schlocko house whom your early novels were rented to in your callow youth, and whom you have no intention of doing business with again, you can always try to make yourself more trouble than you're worth. Be obnoxious. Don't take no for an answer. Threaten lawsuits. Send them voodoo dolls. Convince them that you're crazy. All the while screaming "Let My People Go."

After all, if they don't intend to republish the book anyway, is holding onto it really worth all this shit? And if it is, well then that should convince them to get it back in print, shouldn't it?

Of course, Mr. Hyde will have a hard time doing his number successfully unless Dr. Jekyll has gotten the formula right. Which is to say all this is going to work only if you believe in what you've written. Which is to say that it was important to you when you wrote it. If it was just another piece of yardgoods you reamed out to you, brother, don't expect readers to take it seriously, which means why should anyone want to republish it for posterity?

Which brings us back to virtue, and how you can measure it in your bank balance.

Secret Number Two: In the long run, hackwork doesn't pay.

Reaming out six books a year or writing your own Buck Rogers series, or whatever your particular poison, may run up a lot of quick bread as long as your fingers hold out, but it also means you've got to keep doing it. Because you're just generating income by the sweat of your brow, not accumulating literary capital.

12

Is a good house going to pay you a top advance for a new novel if they know you'll have five others out that year? How valuable will your resale rights be if reissues of your work get crowded out of the racks by your current bumper crop?

If you want your work to be taken seriously, meaning, in our current sphere of discourse, kept in print, then you've got to take it seriously enough yourself. You've got to take it seriously enough to go through the hassle of reversions and resales, which means that you've got to believe you're going to have something worth buying when you've gotten it done.

Perhaps uniquely among the genres of publishing, science fiction novels seem to be subject to and beneficiaries of a rough brand of cosmic justice. They first appear on the stands as a little—though growing—backwater in the flood of new paperback fiction that comes out every month. When the waters recede after a year or two, most of these books are out of print and off the stands. Even most best sellers recede into the dustbin of time with yesterday's hits.

But there are all these weird little bookstores that sell only science fiction and somnolent sf departments in bigger stores where books lay for years, and maybe the best 30 or 40 sf novels in a given year stick around on these shelves, and start reappearing again every couple of years or so in a new package.

Not just the Nebula and Hugo winners and the runners up, but maybe the top 30 or 40 novels of the year. Now come on, surely even those of us obsessed by the competition for Joe's beer money can aspire to writing one of the 30 best sf novels of the year from time to time? If from time to time, why not all the time, like one every year or two?

Sure, you've probably got to spend more time figuring out beforehand where you're going, and maybe write deeper and longer books, and resign yourself to a little rewriting, and yes, your production will probably "suffer."

But even if you've thoroughly convinced yourself that you're just in it for the money, the numbers still come out. Hackwork doesn't pay in the long run.

And we haven't even considered anything outside the domestic market yet. And if a science fiction writer isn't making as much money out of the Great World Out There as he is in the USA, he just isn't doing something right.

NOVEMBER 1979
COLUMN 2

As I write this, I'm fresh off the plane from Paris (or as fresh as I can expect to be after eight hours in the air and six time zones towards morning), after a month in England and France; attending the WorldCon, hanging out, and taking care of business.

Of which there is plenty on the other side of the Atlantic and on the other side of the Pacific too. Those of you who attended the Brighton WorldCon probably already have a good impression of the trans-national readership of today's science fiction. Fans, writers, and editors from all over Europe, and smatterings from Australia and Japan, even a couple of Russians. International media, including even a TV crew from *Temp X*, French National Television's sf fanzine of the air.

Yet while the total readership for science fiction is greater in Europe (not even including the Soviet Union and Japan), than in the U.S., the brute fact is that the lion's share of the science fiction published there is not domestic product but American imports.

Foreign rights to American science fiction contribute significantly to the positive side of the U.S. trade balance, and it should be doing likewise to your credit balance too.

Just as the total readership for science fiction in Europe exceeds the total American readership, it is quite possible for a book written by an American writer to earn more in toto outside the American market than within it. In France, for example, I have had a science fiction novel (*Bug Jack Barron*) sell in the neighborhood of 20,000 copies in an expensive trade edition which stayed in print even after the mass market paperback came out and that could easily end up selling 100,000 copies. *Swiss book club rights*, fer chrissakes, were worth $600 on the French edition. While this is admittedly near the top end of what is usually possible, it is not the French equivalent of *Dune* or *Lord of the Rings*. And those would be good numbers on an American publisher's royalty statements. One country, and we're already talking about maybe $15,000 or $20,000.

And the thing is, there are three or four markets of that size in Europe, another in Japan, and enough more minor markets to add up, too. *The Iron Dream* sold 40,000 copies in England in its first edition—high, but not outrageously so. *The Solarians*, certainly not one of my major works, has earned me maybe $5,000 in Italy. German advances commonly top $2,000, and since the death of Franco, Spanish rights prices have been moving into the same neighborhood, along with the Japanese, since the advent of a large greeting card publisher into Japanese sf publishing. Portuguese, Scandinavian, Dutch, and Greek rights can aggregate another few thousand, though you won't get rich on them.

Advances in Europe tend to be low in relation to the eventual royalty earn-out. But given a kosher contract (which is by no means always the case), you'll get your royalties above the advance down through the years with regularity and honesty.

Certainly foreign rights should account for at least a third of the income of any successful American science fiction writer who is getting his fair share, and just as certainly, foreign rights have been much more important than that to more than one American sf writer in economic adversity.

Question is, how do you get a handle on all this? If you have an American agent with good foreign rights coverage, you're in the best possible position already, because, after all, we're talking about maybe ten different countries here, each with its own way of doing business, and the ideal solution is to have experts in each doing it for you.

Those American agents who do have good foreign rights coverage work through sub-agents in the various countries. Thus your work is being handled by French agents in France, German agents in Germany, Italian agents in Italy, and so forth. This is why the usual commission on foreign rights is 20% and not 10%— the American agent is not in business for his health and the foreign agents must get their commission too.

Of course, not all American agents have good access to this international network, and not all selling American sf writers have American agents in the first place.

So what to do if your foreign rights aren't being maximally handled through an American agent?

Well, your friendly American publisher has a suggestion for you on many standard contracts. Most American publishers will be happy to sell your foreign rights for you.

Sometimes this is a good idea and sometimes it is not. For one thing, not all American publishers have aggresssive foreign rights coverage, and for another, the "commission" they take varies from 20% to 50%. Further, this percentage, whatever it is, isn't always treated like a commission. Your part may be written off against the unearned American advance. Even if it is not, it could take you a long time to get your royalties. Some American publishers forward your foreign rights money within 30 or 60 days of receipt, but others hold it over for the next royalty statement, which could mean you don't get it for over a year after the foreign publisher shelled it out to the foreign sub-agent.

So letting an American publisher handle your foreign rights is very much an individual question and one which calls for close reading and careful negotiation of the relevant clauses in the contract. In general, if you are unagented, or if your American agent isn't really doing much with your foreign rights, if the publisher is taking no more than 20%, and if the foreign proceeds are not accounted against your American advance and are forwarded to you within 90 days of receipt by the publisher, having your publisher be your foreign rights agent is probably the way to go.

Or course, you could always change American agents and seek one who will deliver a proper-sized foreign income. The ability to handle foreign rights should certainly be a major factor in your choice of agent.

But maybe you don't have an agent, or you like the one you have even though he isn't delivering foreign sales, and your publisher wants 40%. What do you do then?

Well, you can try to plug into the international sf agent network through a different channel. Some English agents have very close working relationships with agents on the Continent, and these will be willing to handle your translation rights as well as your British rights. You can run your foreign rights through a British "master agent" instead of an American one while retaining your American agent for domestic purposes.

Or you can go a slower but ultimately perhaps most interesting and rewarding route and seek out separate agents in the individual foreign markets yourself. This is certainly not easy, and keeping it together yourself will be time-consuming and correspondence-creating: but there is one large advantage— namely that you will pay only a 10% commission to your foreign agents, with no one else getting that extra 10% but you.

I hasten to add that I do not do this. With the exception of British rights, for complicated and semi-personal reasons, my foreign rights have always been handled by my American agents. However, in the last few years, I have become convinced of the positive value of beginning to get to know the foreign agents and editors on more of a one-to-one level, relating to them as one would to their American counterparts.

After all, your work *is* reaching a whole other world out there—in fact, not one but several. Different books get different receptions in different countries and different possibilities arise. If you can keep in tune with what is happening in those other worlds, irrespective of who is handling your rights and how, you may learn, for example, that there is a whole line of single-author collections in France, or that it might be worth your while to take a trip to Britain when your next book comes out there, or that you are the most popular science fiction writer in Luxembourg.

Aside from the bank balance, an international perspective on your work can be good for the head. You will find the level of criticism of sf much higher in England and France than in the U.S., good enough in some cases to tell you things you really didn't know about your own stuff. You will also find that patterns of sales and popularity differ widely from country to country. Space opera is where it's at in Germany right now, but not in France, where Philip K. Dick is bigger than Tolkien or the Conan Combine.

You will also find, in general, people pleased to make the actual acquaintance of a writer they are handling or publishing, and people pleased, too, to have their importance in the total publishing of your ouvre rightfully acknowledged.

Indeed, if anything, the most discomforting thing about contact with the science fiction scenes in European countries is that you are likely to find yourself being made much of, somewhat at the expense of the indigenous sf writers.

In part, this is an Anglo-American linguistic failing—every foreign sf publisher has an editor who can read and evaluate novels in English, but few American or British houses have editors capable of evaluating books in French or Dutch or German, etc. In part, this is just a narrower example of the way English tends to dominate international mass media.

But there is also an attitude in some European quarters that American, and to a lesser extent, British sf is the real stuff, the cutting edge, and that most of the domestic product is second-rate or derivative. Whether this is true or not is something that, alas, I am totally incompetent to judge, since like most Britishers and Americans, I am far from fluently multilingual.

Suffice to say that this *is* the situation, and while it may not redound to the benefit of Continental writers, it sure as shit can make life easier for bloated American sf plutocrats. For the American sf writer, the karma is sweet. The question of paying it back may be the subject of a future column.

MARCH 1980
COLUMN 6

Early on in this series of columns, I opined that since Anglophone sf wás enriching British and American writers in non-English-speaking countries, we Anglophone sf writers had a certain karmic debt to discharge re our non-English-writing brethren. Not that we're ripping them off, which we are not, but that the science fiction communtiies in other countries have been very generous to us, and that it would be nice to repay the favor. Not that I had very many bright ideas at the time either, or that I have any terrific answers now. But at least the subject should be raised for discussion.

For one thing, compared to us, non-Anglophone sf writers are somewhat up against the wall. These days it *is* possible for American sf writers to live off their domestic rights, and British writers of enterprise can sell their books in the U.S. and be in the same position. For us, an advance of a few thousand dollars from France or Italy or Spain is a nice langinappe, but if you're writing in French or Italian or Spanish, you have to live off it. Your chances of cracking the English-language market are next to nil currently.

And that's where the big money is.

Sure, you can sell your English-language sf readily in six or seven countries and end up with a total foreign advance that equals or surpasses what American rights went for. But only because you're being translated into all of the languages of sf. And that's happening because you're originating your work in English.

It is a plain fact of life that English dominates the international media, and international sf publishing even more so. The Anglophone market embraces northward of 350,000,000 people, and no other market for sf approaches even a third of that, excluding the Soviet Union, which is a separate case. You'll get a lot of argument from the French, among others, if you claim that modern sf is an Anglo-American invention, but no one at all can argue against the proposition that English-language sf has the highest international profile.

Foreign publishers stay up on the latest Anglophone sf, and they're eager to publish the well-known titles. Why shouldn't they be? They can pick books that have already proved their way in the biggest sf market of the world. While translation is an additional cost, translators are notoriously underpaid, and they can frequently get an Anglophone novel for less than a domestic novel of similar level because the locals know their own market conditions better than we do and because we don't have French or Spanish or Italian or German as the language of our primary income.

Thus does English dominate the sf market in non-Anglophone countries. Some foreign editors contend that English-language sf is simply better on the average than the local product. Unfortunately most of us, myself included, have no way of knowing. But even if this is so, it may as much be an effect of the commercial situation as a cause. At two or three or four grand a book—or even less—the non-Anglophone writer either has to churn it out like a demon or resign himself to writing on a part-time basis. Sound familiar to any of you old pros?

Now, of course, if these European sf writers could turn around and sell their work in the U.S. and Britain, we would no longer be benefitting at their expense. We'd be selling in their country and they'd be selling in ours and we might even be able to pool information so that we all knew the international market conditions better and could be sure we got the best we could everywhere.

From publishers' points of view, the numbers are interesting. You can pay a French novelist, for example, more money for the American rights to his sf novel than the advance he got in his own country and still be getting the book cheap by your standards. True, you have to pay for a translation, but even after that you're still not laying out big bucks. If you choose only top-of-the-line foreign sf novels, you can get yourself a book with built-in good reviews to put on the cover to use as a linc-leader for the cost of a middle-list book. If you choose middling foreign novels, you can get them *real* cheap.

The problem of course is how in hell do you know which books to acquire? You certainly can't afford to have mere *submissions* translated. In foreign countries, all sf houses have someone who can evaluate sf novels in English, but there's no way any American house has the personnel to evaluate books in half a dozen languages. I wonder how many sf editors in the U.S. and Britain read in any second language at all.

Of course in theory non-Anglophone writers or publishers could pay for translations and submit to American and British publishers in English, but this is an economic lunacy unless you're assured of a sale up front.

Is there any solution?

Well, Don Wolheim (at DAW) seems to have at least a partial

solution somewhere, whatever it is. He's published occasional French work from time to time, done, I think, a book that was originally in Swedish, one or two German works, several Russians, and even succeeded in making the Strugatski brothers "Names" in English. So apparently it can be done. Maybe Don can read some of these languages. Maybe he has some people working for him who can. Maybe he should let us know how he does it.

Now I don't think that even Don Wolheim would characterize himself as the last of the big spenders. If DAW is doing this, it must be an economically viable proposition. After all, why shouldn't it be? Let's face it, with so many sf titles being published, middle-range books shouldn't be such stiff competition for the cream from some other country.

What can other sf publishers do to get in on this? Probably something like what Don Wolheim does, whatever it is. You don't even have to know what it is, because it's probably something unique and idiosyncratic to his situation. So you look for something like that in your situation.

Maybe as an editor you do read one other language. Maybe your assistant or an ambitious secretary does. If so, you can rely to a certain extent on their judgment without sacrificing your own.

After all, the book you're going to sell is the English translation. Your foreign-language reader can certainly tell you what you need to know about the story and characters. Unlike a portion-and-outline submission, you know that the finished work is not going to deviate from this. And the quality of the writing is, after all, the quality of the translator's prose in English which you *can* judge first-hand.

Now I'm not suggesting that there is going to be, or should be, an avalanche of sf novels translated into English. For one thing, far fewer sf novels are written in each non-Anglophone country, and for all I know, maybe the average quality of the domestic product *is* lower. But surely there must be a dozen or two non-English sf novels written in the rest of the world each year which would be worthy and economically viable candidates for English-language publication.

So what we are really talking about is a series of special cases. One publisher, for example, might develop a French capability. This house would first seek submissions from French sf writers at large, and then, when there were some numbers, knowledge, and track records, establish continuing relationships with selected French writers of its choice whose work it can have some reliance upon up front.

Another house might go through the same process with Italian sf writers or German sf writers as DAW and Macmillan seem to be doing with the Russians.

From the other side, what can non-Anglophone writers, editors, and publishers do about getting a piece of the lucrative Anglophone market? Well, for one thing, foreign publishers can seek out some kind of relationship with an American house. If you're a French publisher who happens upon that one American house which somehow has a capability to evaluate fiction in French, you're not only ahead of the game in the U.S., you make yourself much more attractive to the most desirable French writers. Maybe you can ferret out an American house that has a *potential* for evaluating books in your language but which has been unaware of the possibility or the profits.

The same, of course, goes for writers. Obviously, if you run into an American editor who's willing to take a submission in your language, you've solved the problem. So if and when such possibilities reveal themselves, non-Anglophone writers should pool their information, and everyone should let everyone else know when they find such a potential somewhere.

Beyond that, the non-Anglophone sf community might try to come forward with its own evaluation services for the English-speaking market. Foreign editors, critics, and agents who are fluent in English might try to establish contact and eventual trust with some Anglophone publisher to the point where *they* could be the evaluators for the Anglophone publishers of sf written in their native language.

The foreign "agent" of an American pubisher would first of all serve as the slushpile reader so that the obvious duds would be disposed of quickly and easily. That would leave the books that fit within the parameters of the American publisher, a manageable number of books.

Part of the job for this foreign "agent" might be to build up a network of translators. These would regularly read the good possibilities, looking for something they would want to translate. The foreign editor would know who was good at what kind of translation and what book would be best done by whom. When book and potential translator were put together, the translator would then write his pitch in English for the American publisher, much like a portion-and-outline proposal.

On this basis, the American publisher could issue a contract, with as much or more assurance of getting what was expected as on a standard portion-and-outline deal.

It requires translators to be willing to do some amount of work on spec, but not a whole translation, and in return it offers them a chance to help hustle up their own work.

Well, that's about my best thinking on the subject, and whether it will result in anything is problematical. Please, nobody out there ask me to act as your agent! If there are American publishers who are interested in any of this, I'll be glad to define your interest in this book. If I can put you in touch with a congruent non-Anglophone counterpart, I'm willing to go that far. But please, don't foreign publishers and editors ask me to ferret out American contacts for them. That is further than I have the time or the knowledge to go right now.

THE SFWA MODEL PAPERBACK CONTRACT

AGREEMENT made this _____ day of _____ , 19 _____
between _____ ,
whose residence address is _____
(hereinafter called the Author); and _____ ,
whose principal place of business is at _____
(hereainafter called the Publisher); with respect to a work now
entitled _____
(hereinafter called the Work)

WITNESSETH:

In consideration of the mutual covenants herein contained, the
parties agree as follows:

1. GRANT
    The Author grants to the Publisher for a period of five (5) years
from the date of first publication the sole and exclusive right to
publish and sell an English language paperback edition of the Work
throughout the United States, its territories and possessions, and
Canada. Upon the expiration of this agreement five (5) years from
the date of original publication, the Publisher shall have first option
to conclude an agreement with the Author for continued publication
rights to the Work on terms to be mutually agreed upon. Should no
such agreement be concluded within sixty (60) days of the expiration of this agreement, all rights to the Work shall automatically
revert to the Author.

2. REPRESENTATIONS AND WARRANTIES
    The Author warrants and represents that this Work is original
with him and has not heretofore been published in paperback form,
that he is sole author and proprietor of said Work with full power
and right to enter into this agreement and to grant the rights hereby
conveyed to the Publisher; that said Work contains no matter which
is libelous and infringes no right or privacy or copyright; that he has
not heretofore and will not hereafter during the term of this
agreement enter into any agreement or understanding which would
conflict with the rights herein granted the Publisher. If the Author
shall breach this warranty, the Publisher shall be entitled to
injunctive relief in addition to all other remedies which may be
available to it. The Author further agrees that he will hold the
Publisher, its distributors, and any retailer harmless against re-
covery or penalty finally sustained arising out of his breach of this
warranty, and in this event he will reimburse the Publisher for all
court costs and legal fees incurred. Any out of court settlement of
any suit filed jointly against the Author and the Publisher shall be
made only by mutual agreement in writing between same.

3. ADVANCE
    Subject to the provisions hereof, the Publisher agrees to pay the
Author as advance against royalties to be earned at the rate
hereinafter set forth the sum of $_____ payable as follows:
    $_____ on the Author's signing of this agreement.
    $_____ on acceptance by the Publisher of the Author's com-
            pleted manuscript of said work.

4. ROYALTIES

The Publisher will pay the Author royalties based upon net sales as reported by the Publishers distributors as follows: On copies sold at the full retail price as imprinted on the cover: ___% of said retail price on the first one hundred thousand (100,000) copies sold and ___% thereafter. On all other copies sold at special rates, through book clubs, or as remainders, a percentage of the per copy amount received by the Publisher equal to sixty percent (60%) of the percentage of the per copy amount received by the Author under the minimum royalty rate for regular sales , or five percent (5%) of net proceeds to the Publisher, whichever shall be greater.

5. SUBSIDIARY RIGHTS

The Author and/or his agent shall retain in full the exclusive right to sell or license the Work for publication in whole or in part, in English or in any foreign language, in any way, shape, edition, or form not in conflict with the rights granted to the Publisher under this agreement, and shall further retain the full and exclusive rights to license the Work for use in other media, except that the Publisher shall have the right to license second serial rights subsequent to book publication, and shall retain fifty percent (50%) of the proceeds of such licensing or sale.

Upon mutual agreement between the Publisher and the Author, the Publisher may act as the Author's agent in any subsidiary rights matter, in which event the Publisher shall receive ten percent (10%) of the amount paid and the Author shall receive ninety percent (90%). However the legal right to make agreements for subsidiary rights, licensing or sale shall remain with the author.

6. STATEMENTS AND PAYMENTS

The Publisher shall forward to the Author or his agent royalty statements to be computed as of June 30 and December 31 of each year of this agreement within thirty (30) days following such respective dates along with any payments indicated to be due thereby.

The Author shall have the right to examine or cause his duly appointed representatives to examine the accounts of the Publisher at any time after written demand by the Author. In the event discrepancies between the royalty statements and the Publisher's accounts shall total more than one hundred dollars ($100.00) in the Author's favor under this and any other agreements between the Author and the Publisher, the Publisher shall tender such moneys due to the Author within ten (10) days, along with reimbursement in full for any duly verified expenses incurred by the Author as a result of the auditing procedure. Should such discrepancies total less than one hundred dollars ($100.00) in favor of the Author, the Publisher shall tender such money due to the Author within ten (10) days, but shall not be liable for reimbursement of the Author's expenses.

7. MANUSCRIPT AND DELIVERY

The Author agrees to deliver to the Publisher on or before _____ and in final revised form an English language manuscript of approximately _____ words.

If the Author shall fail to deliver said manuscript to the Publisher within the time herein provided, or having delivered same shall otherwise breach this agreement, the Author shall thereupon, on demand, repay to the Publisher all sums advanced to him under this agreement.

If, in the opinion of the Publisher, the manuscript is unacceptable or unsatisfactory to the Publisher, the Publisher may reject it by written notice within thirty (30) days of delivery, in which case any sums previously advanced to the Author under this agreement shall be retained by the Author, this agreement shall be deemed terminated and there shall be no further obligation upon the Publisher to publish said Work or to make any further payment hereunder, and all rights granted to the Publisher under this agreement shall revert to the Author.

8. EDITING RIGHTS

No changes, additions, deletions, abridgements, or condensations in the text of the Work or changes of title shall be made by the Publisher, its agents, or employees, without the expressed, itemized, and specific written consent of the Author. Prior to setting of type, final copyedited version of manuscript shall be submitted to the Author.

9. GALLEYS AND PROOFS

Prior to publication the Pubisher upon advance notification shall provide the Author with galley proofs of the Work, which the Author shall correct and return to the Publishers within twenty (20) days of receiving same. The expense of the Author's proof corrections exceeding ten percent (10%) of composition costs shall be charged against the Author's royalties hereunder, except that any such correction resulting from the Publisher's failure to faithfully reproduce the text of the manuscript as delivered by the Author shall in no case be charged against the Author's royalty account.

Prior to the printing of the book jacket of the Work, the Publisher shall submit to the Author a proof or other facsimile of the jacket text and design for his approval, which shall not be unreasonably withheld.

10. PUBLICATION

The Publisher is hereby authorized and mandated to secure copyright to the Work in the name of the Author, to arrange for sale of said Work in Canada simultaneously with first sale in the United States, and to fulfill all other obligations necessary to protect copyright to the Work under United States law and the International Copyright Convention.

11. PUBLICATION

The Publisher agrees to publish and commence distribution of said Work within twelve (12) months of approval and acceptance of the Author's final manuscript. In the event the Publisher shall fail to publish and distribute the Work by said date, this agreement shall terminate forthwith, and all rights hereunder shall revert to the Author. The Author shall retain any payments made to him under this agreement, without forfeiting his rights to seek further damages from the Publisher. However, this mandated publication date may be extended to any other date, and any number of extensions may be made, upon mutual agreement between the Publisher and the Author.

12. AUTHOR'S COPIES

On publication the Publisher shall give to the Author twenty-five (25) copies of the published Work, which may not be resold. Any further copies desired by the Author may be purchased at fifty percent (50%) of the retail price.

10. INFRINGEMENT

If during the existence of this agreement the copyright shall be infringed, the Publisher may, at its own expense, take such legal action, in the Author's name if necessary, as may be required to restrain such infringement or to seek damages therefor. The Publisher shall not be liable to the Author for the Publisher's failure to take such legal steps. If the Publisher does not bring such an action, the Author may do so, in his name and at his own expense. Money damages recovered for an infringement shall be applied first toward the repayment of the expense of bringing and maintaining the action, and thereafter the balance shall belong to the Author, provided, however, that any money damages recovered on account of a loss of the Publisher's profits shall be divided equally between the Author and the Publisher.

14. BANKRUPTCY AND INSOLVENCY

If a petition in bankruptcy shall be filed by or against the Publisher, or if it shall be judged insolvent by a court, or if a Trustee or a Receiver of any property of the Publisher shall be appointed in any suit or proceeding by or against the Publisher, or if the Publisher shall make an assignment for the benefit of creditors or shall take the benefit of any bankruptcy or insolvency Act, or if the Publisher shall liquidate its business for any cause whatsoever, this agreement shall terminate automatically without notice, and such termination shall be effective as of the date of the filing of such petition, adjudication, appointment, assignment or declaration or commencement of reorganization or liquidation proceedings, and all rights granted hereunder shall thereupon revert to the Author.

15. INHERITANCE

This agreement shall be binding upon and insure to the benefit of the heirs, executors, administrators and assigns of the Author, and upon and to the successors and assigns of the Publisher.

1. GRANT

The wording you see here is not something you will presently see in any paperback publisher's standard contract. What this Model Contract clause is really all about is not the basically pro forma matter of grants but the absolutely vital matter of *reversion*. Some of the sleazier publishers' contracts have no reversion clause at all, which means that the publisher can keep your book out of print for the rest of your life and still retain the right to publish it should there be a film sale or should you develop into a superstar. Unless you are starving to death or have been offered a six-figure advance, *never* sign a contract without a reversion clause. Without a proper reversion clause, you are in effect transferring de facto ownership of your book from yourself to your publisher. Lest you think that this is merely a matter of pride or technicality, let me point out that I have resold reverted books more than once, and in one case for *double* the original advance. In general, there is no reason for you to let a publisher retain rights he is not exercising. If your book is out of print, you want it back because, if you believe in what you are doing, you must believe that the value of your books will increase as your career progresses. If the publisher is not enhancing this capital gain by keeping your book in print, why should he reap the later benefit?

Most paperback contracts *do* have reversion clauses. The standard arrangement is that if your book is out of print five years after date of publication, you write the publisher a letter pointing it out and requesting that he put it back into print. If he does not, the book reverts to you in six more months.

There is a Catch-22 here, however: the words "out of print." Most contracts define this only vaguely. What it usually boils down to is that as long as the publisher has any books in the warehouse—even only a hundred copies—the book is not out of print and the reversion clause is worthless. I have in the past gotten around this by getting a publisher to accept a different definition of "out of print." In the past, most royalty statements had figures for number of books printed, copies sold, returns, and "copies yet to be accounted for." When a royalty statement showed a "copies yet to be accounted for" figure of zero, or when sales plus returns equalled the number of books printed, which amounted to the same thing, then the publisher was admitting right on the royalty statement that there were no more books available for sale (since paperback returns consist of the covers ripped off books and sent back by the distributors for credit) and the book was as out of print as anything could be.

Now, however, many publishers are wising up. Their royalty statements no longer give you a figure for returns or "copies yet to be accounted for" and some of them no longer even tell you the print run. Which means it is no longer possible to prove that your book is out of print by referring to your royalty statement. (More on all this when we get to the STATEMENT AND PAYMENTS clause.)

So this is why, for purpose of the Model Paperback Contract—which is meant to advocate the ideal situation from the writer's point of view—the reversion clause has been eliminated entirely and the subject is dealt with up front in the GRANT clause. The wording in the Model Contract does not come entirely from left field. A five-year grant of paperback rights which automatically expires without reference to in print or out of print is what many hardcover houses give to paperback houses and which many paperback houses customarily accept from hardcover publishers. If a paperback house will give this deal to a hardcover house, why not to a writer? Especially since paperback houses these days are trying to convince writers that paperback original publication is as good as a hardcover deal. Sad to say, I know of no writer who has yet succeeded in getting this GRANT clause written into a contract, but this is a Model Contract and at least this clause can serve as a bargaining position in getting better definitions of "out of print" in standard reversion clauses.

2. REPRESENTATIONS AND WARRANTIES

This is basically the standard publishers' wording, with a few *very* important differences. The publisher certainly has a right to be guaranteed by the author that the rights he is buying are in fact free, that the book is not a piece of plagiarism or libel, and that the author will not turn around and resell it to another publisher as soon as he has cashed the check. *However,* the standard publishers' wording also has the author guaranteeing that the work contains no obscene material and holds the author entirely responsible for the consequences of any obscenity prosecution or suit. Since these days no one really knows what is legally obscene or not and since definitions vary crazily from jurisdiction to jurisdiction, and since publishers retain lawyers who can go over manuscripts before they are published, this should be *their* responsibility, not yours. Try to strike out any references to obscenity and the like from publishers' contracts. This is probably not important enough to blow a deal over, but it is certainly worth a try, and this is a point that some writers *have* won in negotiations with publishers.

In the standard publishers' wording of this clause, the author gets stuck for all settlements, court costs, legal fees and penalties arising out of any suit against the publisher or the publisher and the author jointly. This stinks. It means that if some crank sues the publisher for libel and loses, the author gets screwed for court costs and legal fees. The standard publishers' wording also gives the publisher de facto power of attorney to handle all legal actions as he sees fit, including the unilateral right to make out-of-court settlements. This stinks worse. It means that the publisher can decide to get rid of a worthless and groundless nuisance libel suit by giving the crank a couple thousand dollars of *your* money.

The final sentence of the Model Contract WARRANTY clause takes care of this by mandating that the author must agree to any out-of-court settlement. The second-to-last sentence inserts the words "finally sustained" between the author's obligation to reimburse everyone under the sun for penalties arising out of an action and his obligation to pay court costs and legal fees. What this means is that if the publisher *loses* in court because of the author's libel, plagiarism or other breach of warranty, the author pays the judgment and the court costs, which seems only fair; but he doesn't get stuck for anything, court costs included, if it turns out that the suit is worthless, that in fact he hasn't done anything wrong.

Negotiating changes in this clause with a publisher is a son of a bitch, because you end up arguing with the legal eagles who wrote his version, who are usually sons of bitches when it comes to having their wording changed. However, editors don't pay too much attention to this kind of stuff, so what you can try is simply crossing out all references to obscenity, typing in the last sentence of the Model Contract clause concerning out-of-court settlements at the end of their standard boilerplate, and sticking in the words "finally sustained" in the appropriate place in the court costs and legal fees subclause. Don't negotiate it, just do it without calling anyone's attention to it. It's maybe a fifty-fifty chance that it will simply slip by if the legal department doesn't review the final version of the contract.

However, my advice is to forget about it if the editor gives you flack for writing it. Pretend innocence, tell him you just thought those changes were standard, and give in unless you don't care that much about blowing the sale. The standard publishers' wording of this clause stinks, but you can't win an argument with his legal department on points of law. But nothing ventured, nothing gained.

3. ADVANCE

This is more or less the standard advance clause you'll find in most kosher paperback contracts. There are only two non-kosher variations you may run into. Some publishers may want to split the advance three ways: a sum on signing, a sum on acceptance, and a third sum on publication. I see no real reason why a publisher should hold on to a third of the money *that you've already done all your work for* until they finally bring out the book, maybe as long as 18 months or more later, collecting interest on *your* money all the while. An exception would be when the advance is really large; it enables them to spread the expense over two or even three fiscal years, and it also enables the writer to spread the income tax on the large sum over two or three years, too, at some savings. Another exception would be the resale of a reverted work where you've already been paid once for all the work you've done; from the publisher's point of view, a reissue is a marginal enterprise anyway, so it is politic not to make waves.

The other non-kosher variation is a bit more serious. Some publishers want the contract to call for the author to repay the signature advance if they reject the completed book. While it is certainly reasonable for the publisher to get the signature advance back if the author doesn't deliver the completed manuscript on time, since the author will then have breached the contract, the author has *not* breached the contract if the publisher happens not to like what he has turned in. Since all contracts give the publisher the right not to publish the completed book without having to justify the decision, the author should not be financially liable for a publisher's decision over which he has no control. It is marginally acceptable for the advance clause to call for repayment of the signature advance in the event that the author resells the book to another publisher, but beyond that, any repayment clause is really unfair.

As to what constitutes an acceptable paperback advance, the variation is now enormous. The highest paperback advance for a science-fiction novel now on record is $500,000, which does not mean that figures in the $4000 to $7500 range are necessarily rip-offs. Some houses still pay $2000 to $3000 for a first or even second novel.

4. ROYALTIES

The SFWA Model Paperback Contract does not specify any royalty rates because these vary widely according to the strength of the author's bargaining position. In general, once a book sells a certain number of copies, further royalties are paid at a higher rate, since by this "break point," the publisher has already made a handsome profit and his unit costs are reduced. Most publishers' contracts set the break point at 150,000 copies, but the Model Contract sets it as 100,000 copies because it is sometimes possible to negotiate this lower figure.

As to acceptable royalty percentages, a few years ago the minimum was 4% on the first 150,000 copies and 6% thereafter. Anything less than this is total robbery. Today, the acceptable minimums are 6% and 8%, though a first novelist in a weak bargaining position might conceivably have to settle for 4% and 6% from certain of the sleazier houses. More than a few writers in relatively strong bargaining positions have been able to get 8% and 10%, and a few have even gotten as much as a straight 10% on all copies sold. If you're William Peter Blatty or Harold Robbins or maybe Arthur C. Clarke, you might even be able to squeeze out 12% and 15%, but don't hold your breath.

The final, somewhat confusing sentence of this clause takes some fancy explaining. Publishers sell their books to distributors at a 40% discount, so if the cover price for a book is $1.00, the publisher grosses 60¢ and the author's royalty, at 10%, is 10¢. So the most the publisher collects on *any* such book is 60¢, not $1.00. Therefore, since the publisher's end is 60% of the cover price, the author should not have his royalty rate reduced beyond the percentage of the cover price that the publisher is discounting in a special sale or remainder. That is, royalties should be reduced proportionally to the reduction in the publisher's end of the gross only, not proportionally to the total gross, since the publisher gives away 40% to begin with on normal sales. The 5% of net proceeds floor is in there to preclude any fancy bookkeeping hanky-panky on the part of the publisher by setting some kind of minimum for royalties under any reduced cover price sale.

5. SUBSIDIARY RIGHTS

This clause in the Model Contract is not exactly your ordinary publishers' wording. Many publishers' contracts give the *publisher* control of all subsidiary rights—British rights, movie rights, serial rights, etc. These contracts usually attempt to split the proceeds 50-50. If you sign one of these, not only must you split the subsidiary rights proceeds with the publisher, but the publisher usually holds onto *your* end of the take for a full royalty period after the money comes in. Still further, some publishers will then apply your end of the subsidiary rights money to any unearned advance outstanding on their edition of your book so it can be years before you see any of the money, if ever. This can amount to a lot of bread, more than the original American advance for foreign sales alone. On two of my books, for example, the total foreign rights income has been three or four times the original American advance, and the Science Fiction Book Club does pick up paperback originals, and can earn you $3000 and up.

With the exception of book club rights, most publishers will give you back total control and total income on all subsidiary rights, except possible hardcover reprint, without a fight. *But you have to change the contract.* If you're naive enough to let the standard publishers' subsidiary rights clause stand unamended, they'll be happy to keep quiet and let you give them a piece of *your* money. Tell the editor you want to keep these rights, and that you're changing the contract accordingly. This is one clause over which it is worthwhile to blow a deal if it comes down to it, because it is not only a matter of principle but a matter of money, and probably a lot of it. Science fiction sells very well in Europe and Japan. Even years later, a first novel may bring in thousands worldwide, after your reputation has been made, even if you couldn't sell it abroad when it first came out, as witness: my first novel, *The Solarians,* sold for a lousy $1250 advance in 1965, which at this writing has earned me maybe $4000 abroad.

However, if you don't have an agent, it is not a bad idea to let the publisher act as your agent, since many will have foreign and Hollywood contacts you do not. *Provided,* of course, that the publisher isn't getting a bigger cut than an agent would. In the Model Contract, this is set at the agent's standard 10% for everything, but since some agents take a 20% commission on foreign sales, it would not be untoward to give a publisher 20% to act as your agent if need be.

The last sentence of this clause is important if you do decide to let the publisher act as your agent. It insures that you and not the publisher have final say on all subsidiary sales, sign contracts, *and retain ownership* of these rights. It also keeps your agent-publisher from applying all or part of your 90% of the take against any unearned advance on his editions, since you are not granting him ownership of the rights, but only the power to act as your agent.

6. STATEMENTS AND PAYMENTS

This looks pretty much like a pro forma bookkeeping clause, which it was when the Model Contract was written, but things have changed in the past few years here, and not for the better. A few years ago, most publishers had a 30 day from end of royalty period payment and statement clause in their contracts, but that has now changed radically and in a rather sinister fashion. Now most new contracts let them hold onto *your* money for 90 days, or a full fiscal quarter, collecting and *pocketing* the interest on it all the while. This may not seem significant on a few hundred bucks on your one title, but when you realize that the publishers are doing this with *their entire lists,* and stop to consider the high interest rates for short-term loans these days, this is revealed as a huge six or seven figure rip-off of every published writer in the United States!

What can you, the writer, do about this? Not a fucking thing! The publishers' computers are programmed to cough out royalty statements on this new, unfair 90-day basis, and there's *no way* any individual writer can try to change it back to 30 days without blowing the deal. If anything is ever to be done about this, it must be done on a organizational basis—SFWA, MWA, The Author's Guild, and all the other writers' organziations confronting the publishing industry with a united front. So just grit your teeth and sign it as it is.

One small consolation: those of you who have books contracted for under the old 30-day clause now have your publishers in a multiple breach of those old contracts. Since royalty statements now commonly omit figures for total printing, copies yet to be accounted for, and sometimes even returns, it has become very difficult to prove that a book is out of print when it comes to reversion time. So if you try to get an old book back and get static, you can sweetly point out that the publisher has been in breach of the contract since he adopted the 90-day payment policy, and maybe, therefore, he shouldn't make waves about an honest reversion. I've tried this once, and it's worked.

What with the cryptic royalty statements publishers are sending out these days, the second paragraph in this clause assumes added significance, since the only way to get hard figures on *anything* now may be to examine the publishers' books. Some contracts already have a clause like this in them. If yours doesn't, you should make some attempt to get it written in, but frankly, it isn't worth blowing an otherwise kosher deal over.

7. MANUSCRIPT AND DELIVERY

This is pretty much standard industry wording. The only kicker here is that some publishers' wording of this clause allows them, at least in theory, to recover the signature payment if they bounce the finished book. As detailed elsewhere, sometimes this repayment wording is in the ADVANCE clause, but sometimes its cleverly buried right in here, where you're less likely to notice it. As also detailed elsewhere, this stinks. Since the publisher can reject a completed book without having to justify its action (frequently because they've folded their sf line between the time you contracted for the book and the time you finished it) there is no way an author should be held financially liable for a publisher's decision over which he has no control.

8. EDITING RIGHTS

This clause was written into the original American paperback contract for *Bug Jack Barron* by me after much censorship hassle (*not* with *New Worlds*) on the original British serialization. I had a good editor who had no intention of mucking around with the book, and so he didn't object to me protecting myself from something he had no intention of doing in the first place.

But horror stories abound. Ask John Brunner. In fact, on *Bug Jack Barron,* some cretin free-lance copyeditor rewrote the book line by line. The whole thing had to be reset. Had I *not* written this clause into the contract, the publisher could just have apologized and told me they weren't about to go to the expense of resetting the book. Because the standard publisher's editing rights clause is exactly the reverse of the SFWA Model Contract clause—it gives them total carte blanche to make any changes they damn well please. So if you're doing a book that's unusually long, or uses idiosyncratic form or style, or explicit sex, or anything that may be controversial politically, and if you care about your work, you need the protection of the SFWA wording. At the very least, you shouldn't sit still for wording that gives the publisher total arbitrary control over the final published form of the book.

The last sentence of this clause is basically for the benefit of the publishers. If something *has* been screwed up by the copyeditor, better for you and the publisher that it be caught before type is set.

9. GALLEYS AND PROOFS

Any writer who is too lazy to correct his own proofs (and there do seem to be some) has no one to blame but himself if the published book isn't as he wrote it. This clause protects the writer by requiring the publisher to submit galleys, and it protects the publisher by requiring the writer to proof the galleys within a reasonable time, so the publishing schedule doesn't get screwed up. Requiring the publisher to give the writer advance notification before sending the galleys allows you to organize your schedule so that you can get the work done within the required 20 days. Most contracts already have some clause like this, but it's usually more vaguely worded. This wording seems fairer to both author and publisher and you might not have much difficulty substituting it. Standard publisher's wording charges the author for corrections in excess of 10% of composition costs period, but obviously, if they've made a mess, you shouldn't have to pay for correcting it.

The last sentence is mostly blue sky. We all want jacket approval; we seldom get it. This really doesn't give you jacket veto either, but it is a toe in the door.

10. COPYRIGHT

Most publishers' contracts have a clause more or less like this one. A few substandard contracts still have a blank space after "in the name of." Do not let them type in "the publisher." Not even the sleaziest publisher will object to copyrighting the book in the author's name. Simultaneous publication in Canada is necessary to protect your copyright there under Canadian law for some Byzantine reason, having to do, I think, with the question of importing copies of the American edition. Some publishers' clauses do not require them to fulfill all obligations necessary to protect copyright under the International Copyright Convention. Since you have to be an international publishing lawyer to figure this out yourself, it is not unreasonable to expect the publisher to do so.

11. PUBLICATION

A few substandard publishers' contracts do not have this clause at all. Most do, but they usually give the publisher anywhere from 18 months to as much as three years to get the book out. Three years is ridiculous and totally unacceptable; two years is a bit ludicrous too. The 12-month time limit in the SFWA Model Contract may be considered a bit confining by some publishers, and 18 months is within the realm of reason. Reason is the reason why this clause allows the author and publisher to extend the publication date by mutual consent. Some months are better for publication than others, and you don't want to put the publisher in the position of having to cut your mutual commercial throat in order to protect itself from breach of contract.

Most publishers' clauses have the author forfeiting his right to sue if the agreement is cancelled by reason of publisher's failure to bring the book out on time. Since standard publishers' boilerplate never signs away the publisher's right to sue if the author is in breach, why should you hold them blameless in the event of breach? The publisher's failure to bring the book out on time could result in real damages to you far in excess of the advance you've been paid—for instance, if it kills a possible film deal.

12. AUTHOR'S COPIES

This is standard industry wording. The number of free copies you're entitled to can be as few as 6 or as many as 25. Since this is the SFWA Model Contract, it calls for the maximum. Obviously it is not worth seriously endangering a deal over a few bucks worth of freebies, though.

13. INFRINGEMENT

This is fairly standard wording. It allows the publisher to sue for copyright infringement unilaterally at its own expense, allows the author to do the same, and requires neither to do so, nor does it allow either party to stick the other with legal expenses from such a unilateral suit. Sometimes a copyright infringement may just be an excerpt in a fanzine, for example, where the loss or the recoverable amount will not pay the legal fees, in which case, there's no point in obligating either party to sue. It's obviously fair that whoever forked over the money for legal fees should be fully reimbursed before any settlement or award is divided. Since it is the author whose proprietary copyright has been infringed, he should get the settlement or award money after the legal fees have been paid. However, if the publisher can show that the infringement actually cost it money in terms of lost sales, or even the inability to distribute its edition, it seems fair that both parties should be entitled to shares of any damages recovered.

14. BANKRUPTCY AND INSOLVENCY

A lot of legal gobbledygook, but this clause can be vitally

important. What it basically does is revert the book to the author as soon as a publisher gets involved in bankruptcy or insolvency procedures. What *this* prevents is having the book frozen as an asset of the publisher in the event of bankruptcy. Without this protection, you can be screwed nine ways from Sunday if the publisher goes bankrupt—not only do you become a creditor if you are owed royalties (which means that the royalties can be bankrupted out from under you) but the receivers can resell *your* book as part of the liquidation without paying you a dime. Or the book can be tied up for years in legal proceedings, making it impossible for you to resell it even if the bankrupt original publisher never published it. Things like this *have* happened. Books are still tied up in limbo from the Lancer bankruptcy, and in France, Opta went bankrupt, dragged down by the prior bankruptcy of Marabout, and hundreds of authors have been screwed out of royalties and even, in some cases, their shares of the mass market paperback advances.

15. INHERITANCE

This simply obligates the estate of the author to fulfill the terms of the contract as if it were the author and automatically entitles the author's heirs to collect any monies due as if they were the author. It also obligates any company which may absorb the publisher in any way to fulfill the contract.

PART TWO
MARKET FORCES

I began writing the STAYIN' ALIVE column for Locus in 1979 in the ascending phase of what was then seen as the Great Science Fiction Boom. There had been smaller booms before, followed by busts, but these mostly involved the birth and death of many short-lived magazines, and the entry into and exit out of standard model sf publishing by various houses.

This one was different. With hindsight it can be seen that, despite its ups and downs, it ended up permanently transforming the economic modes, possibilities, pecuniary ranges, and publishing of science fiction in the United States. Not surprising, since it occurred during a period when the publishing industry as a whole was going through structural, economic, and even philosophical changes itself. Indeed, as we shall see in later sections, more than the commercial end of science fiction was permanently transformed by the phenomena, which, in process, seemed like boom and semi-bust, but which, in perspective, turned out to be fundamental change.

Not only do these columns written during this evolution reflect the economic ebbs and flows of the period, they also seem to represent a certain evolution in the emphasis of my own, and perhaps the science fiction community's, concerns. For a long time, the economic parameters of being a science fiction writer had been static, and "Stayin' Alive" meant learning how to best deal with more or less static market conditions. But as market conditions began to evolve, as prior precedents became meaningless, as the situation became more complex, as corporate conglomerates came to dominate publishing, as events in the national economy began to impact on sf publishing, science fiction writers, always concerned in their fiction with the interaction of individual destiny with the total political, technological, economic, and social matrix, began to apply this sort of analytical science fictional thinking to their own evolving relationship with the evolving business end of the genre.

Thus these columns began to concern themselves with the nature and results of the marketing forces at work themselves. This section, as well as the one to follow on ART AND COMMERCE, probably are almost as relevant to the existential position and economic situation of the American writer in general as to that of the science fiction writer. But I think it is no accident that such an analysis should first come forth from a science fiction writer writing for the sf community. Writers build fictional worlds, societies, economies, cultures; in order to be the kind of writer who creates such fiction, one almost has to be the sort of person who has an almost obsessive curiosity about how things really work.

No more so, of course, than when the state of one's own bank account is vitally involved.

In passing, let me note that three of the magazines mentioned in this section—Galileo, UnEarth, and Galaxy—are no longer currently with us. A new magazine called Twilight Zone seems to be doing all right.

Not mentioned in this section is a strange new phenomenon, the "semi-prozine." Science fiction fandom (about which much more in another section) publishes scores, perhaps hundreds, of amateur fan magazines called "fanzines." Over the past few years many of them have actually started paying for fiction and even buying stories from well-established writers. For the most part, these magazines are distributed by subscription only, or by subscription and sale at a few specialty bookstores, and are self-financed on shoe-strings by aspiring fans with no previous editorial experience.

Whatever the general quality of the fiction published in these semi-prozines (and by the nature of things, they are the bottom market for short science fiction), they are perhaps the most unique and amazing testimony to the viability of the sf genre as the last remaining major refuge of the American short story.

When readers who perceive that there aren't enough paying outlets for short fiction actually do something about it, reports of the death of the short story as a non-academic art form must be *greatly exaggerated, at least in this corner of the literary galaxy.*

DECEMBER 1979
COLUMN 3

So far, we have examined career strategies over time—how to get the most bucks out of your existing ouvre in terms of domestic reversions and resales and foreign rights. This time around, and not without some trepidation, I will attempt some musings on the burning and confusing question in the forefront of all our minds, sf writers and publishers alike: What will the traffic bear?

What should you ask in the way of an advance for your new sf novel or novel proposal? How should you go about marketing it? Publisher by publisher submission as in hallowed days of yore? A dramatic and flashy new-fangled auction? Hardcover? Paperback original? Combined hard and soft deal?

Used to be, you knew about what you were going to get, and there was a pattern of submissions you could rely upon to secure yourself the best deal possible within fairly narrow parameters. Back before all these changes, publishers' advances for first novels or middle-range books or the top stuff of the year were more or less standard both within the industry and with a given house. From top market to bottom, the variation was only a few thousand, so you started your submission at the best-paying market and worked your way down until you hit paydirt, secure in the knowledge that this way the first offer you got would be the best you could get, much in the manner of marketing short stories to magazines.

Those days, of course, are gone forever.

Joe Haldeman breaks the $100,000 barrier. Orson Scott Card, without a published novel to his name, makes big five-figure deals. Silverberg tops Haldeman. Heinlein gets half a million. Six-figure Benford deal. Sci-fi scribes bag big bucks.

On the other hand, there are still sf writers of surprising prominence (though the number is mercifully diminishing fast) getting advances that don't top four figures. Some of them are tied into old multi-book contracts, some of them don't have agents, or have the wrong agents, and some of them just seem to have had bad karma thrust upon them. And while a few beginning writers with connections or luck or fairy godfathers are getting higher advances than a lot of established old-timers, most beginning sf novelists right now would be happy to have a $5,000 deal.

What the hell is going on? What should a poor boy do? How to make some systematic sense of all this?

As science fiction writers, we should try to take the long view, and try to prophesize what will shake down, rather than be caught up in the *Locus* headlines of the moment. That is how we make our living when it comes to what we write, isn't it? So it makes sense to apply the same technique to the arena of the marketplace, which is to say, the alien ¬ulture we find ourselves in, the setting for our story.

One thing seems still to be true—in the long run, advances are the extrapolated projection of sales. They reflect the publisher's perception of how much bread the book is going to make for him. If they do not reflect this with some degree of consistency, the publisher is heading for the toilet, and long before he gets there, the writers who are showing all that red ink will be thrown off the sleigh to the wolves.

Okay, let's take one of those $100,000 advances and crank through some numbers. Let's assume a $2.25 paperback with a straight 10% royalty rate, a good ballpark average that makes the arithmetic simple. According to my calculator, this book will have to sell 444,444 copies to earn out its advance. How many science fiction novels have ever sold this many copies? A dozen? Ten? Six?

Gulp!

But wait a minute. We're assuming that the writer's earnout point is the same as the publisher's break even point, and if you believe in that, you probably believe in Uncle Scrooge. Out of each $2.25 retail sale, the publisher collects $1.35. Minus the writer's $.225, leaving the publisher a gross of $1.125. Divide this into $100,000, and you get 88,888 copies that the publisher has to sell to get his money back. Of course, the publisher also has to pay for the cover, and for printing the book, and for overhead. So for the sake of argument, let's be generous and say that the publisher's true cost is double that $100,000 advance, or $200,000. Which means he has to sell about 180,000 copies of a book to reach his real break even point, or an even 200,000 copies to show a minimal profit.

Well now at least we begin to know what we're talking about. What are the chances of a $100,000 sf novel selling 200,000 copies? What chance does a $50,000 sf novel have to sell 100,000 copies? Will a $25,000 sf novel sell 50,000 copies? Will a $12,500 novel sell 25,000 copies? Will a $6000 novel sell 12,000 copies?

Very interesting.

From the above figures, it is obvious that any writer of any standing at all in the sf field should certainly not accept less than $25,000 as an advance. I mean, do you want your book published by a house that in effect would be claiming that they don't expect to sell 50,000 copies? And judging by the figures, not even a neophyte should accept less than say $10,000 as an advance, since any sf novel that sells under 25,000 copies is a disaster. Do you want your first novel published by a house whose offer assumes catastrophe?

These figures, I would suggest, are the floors under the current market. $10,000 for anything publishable, and $25,000 for a novel by a writer whose name or track record indicates that it is likely to sell 50,000 copies.

If these figures stun you, remember that these are 1979 dollars, not 1969 dollars, and that what was then a 95¢ or even a 75¢ book is now going for $2.25. So while inflation takes away with one hand, it makes us favored few richer with the other. Welcome to the New Economics of sf publishing.

But what about the top end? We all know that any competent publisher is going to sell 25,000 copies of any sf novel and will sell 50,000 copies of a novel by a known writer over the standard five-year period of the contract. But what are the chances of selling 200,000 copies or more and justifying one of those six-figure advances?

Here the picture gets more ambiguous. 100,000 copies is something of an exceptional get-out for an sf novel, even a monthly paperback lead. Certainly not out of the question, but the publisher is going to have to spend a little something on advertising and promotion to do it, say $5000 to $10,000 on a few ads in the trades, and maybe some posters or stuff. Given an average return rate of 40% to be on the high side, this means that, even figuring in the advertising and promotion budget, the publisher will make money paying an advance of $25,000 for any book they have real enthusiam for. Given the residual sales over the life of the contract, $35,000 is not an unreasonable advance for any book intended to be a properly done monthly lead.

However, as we go up the advance ladder, advertising and promotion gets more important. To justify an advance in the $50,000 to $60,000 range, you're talking about getting out about 170,000 books and selling about 100,000. In the real world, this means more advertising, and the question is whether this can be cost-effective. To hit *Omni* and *Heavy Metal* and *Starlog* and *Future* and *Analog* and *F&SF* and *Locus* and *Starship* and

Publisher's Weekly and really do it up brown costs bucks, and probably in the neighborhood of $25,000 or $30,000. Which means that the publisher's true break even point is going to be about 150,000 sales. For a $100,000 advance, the break even point will be something like 250,000 or 300,000 sales.

The question then becomes whether an advertising program of significant size can break an sf novel out of the high end of the category sales pattern. Once advances climb above about $35,000, you need something beyond an excellent selling science fiction novel to show a profit. A successful monthly sf paperback lead is certainly worth a $35,000 advance, but much beyond that figure, the book must break out into terra nova.

So what *kind* of sf novel can be turned into what kind of break-out book? Well obviously, a movie tie-in like ALIEN or STAR TREK or CLOSE ENCOUNTERS. Obviously, a novel by Arthur Clarke or Isaac Asimov or Ray Bradbury or Frank Herbert.

Beyond the obvious, the situation is still too new for the figures to be in. But one can look at the advertising media a break-out book has to be targeted through and come up with some tentative demographics. My guess is that break-out books will be books whose ads in places like *Omni, Heavy Metal* and *Starlog* will be cost-effective. What kind of books are those?

Well, in *Omni,* we have about a million readers who are part of what I would call the upper fringe of the extended sf readership. They're interested in speculative science. They're also interested in pseudo or fringe science. They're not hard-core sf readers, but they have some familiarity with the stuff and they'll buy an sf novel from time to time. A fairly well-educated and sophisticated bunch of adults who will buy sf novels that represent the upper end of the literary sf spectrum and, perhaps most important, that are accesible to the casual reader.

In *Starlog, Future,* and *Heavy Metal,* we have a younger audience of similar size, the lower fringe of the extended sf readership, kids who are really into sf imagery, films, and comics, but who on the whole are probably not heavy readers of sf prose fiction. They will probably buy novels that closely approximate the spirit and level of sophistication of media sf, but as they mature over the next few years, they will become upwardly mobile. Again, we find ourself confronted with the illusive concept of accessibility.

Simplistically put, what I mean by an accessible novel is a science fiction novel that will be immediately comprehensible to one or both of these extended readerships even if it is the first sf novel that the *Omni* or *Starlog* reader has bought. Something whose imagery, and setting, and concept are not alien (or not too alien) to the frames of reference of the inexperienced sf reader.

On the schlock end of the spectrum, this can be a novel that successfully aspires to mimic a film novelization. On the other end of the spectrum, it can be a novel that begins in the everyday world of the readers' consciousness and smoothly transports them to another time and space, taking nothing for granted. Or something so well written that it accomplishes the same thing by sheer tour de force. Or somehow, a work of diabolic genius that does all three.

So what kind of advance should you seek for your next science fiction novel? Prudence would dictate an advance based loosely upon publishers' true break even points. For the ordinary first or second novel, about $10,000. For a book that you honestly believe can be one of the top 40 of the year, which is to say a monthly lead, $25,000 to $35,000. Beyond that, you have to try to assess your own work in somewhat ruthless commercial terms. Quality aside, is this the kind of novel that, properly published, and properly advertised, will break out of the upper end of the category sales pattern?

And, of course, will the publisher who is making you this six-figure offer actually publish the book properly and throw at least $25,000 into advertising?

Now, from other quarters may come the advice to take the money and run. There is something to be said for this, I suppose, depending on your immediate cash need. Personally, I'd rather take a $35,000 advance on a book that later justifies a $100,000 advance than take a $100,000 advance on a book that ends up justifying only a $35,000 advance. In the first situation, I'd be able to ask $100,000 for the next book, but in the second situation, I'd obviously have some trouble selling the next book at all.

Think of yourself as a baseball player who signs this year's contract on the basis of last year's performance. If you were a bargain last year, you can get the big bucks this year with no sweat. But if you got paid $100,000 to hit .300 and only hit .265, your option just may not be picked up.

This is the way it works in the major leagues, friends, and the major leagues is where science fiction is headed.

First an update on a previous column, the one on the new economics of science fiction and what the traffic should bear in the way of advances. Since that column was written, there has been a slight softening of the market, as the sf boom seems to be leveling off for a while and the long-predicted recession may be beginning to take hold. Dell and Ace have cut back somewhat on their paperback lines, and Berkley has cut back on their hardcovers. The paperback rights to *Lord Valentine's Castle* went for the $75,000 floor instead of setting a new record—not that this is exactly chickenfeed.

What is happening? Well, for one thing, even as I intimated, $100,000 may be a slightly unrealistic advance for a science fiction novel, and the publishers may be realizing this as some of the figures on previous books come in. From the point of view of writers in general, this may not be an entirely bad thing. One of the reasons there have been some list cutbacks is that the bottom couple of books on some lists haven't been doing too well. Part of the reason for this just might be those six-figure books, which, of course, gobble up most of their month's ad budget and then some, leaving general list promotion a bit strapped. Another part of the reason may be the entry of Pocket Books at four books a month. Rack space for science fiction may have reached a temporary saturation point, meaning that increases in the list of one publisher may just eventually cause compensatory decreases elsewhere. And let's face it, folks, the huge and sudden boom in demand for sf novels on the part of publishers may have caused more turkeys to be published than in a period where publishers could pick and choose.

This is not to say that things are going bust. But some adjustments to the new position of science fiction book publishing may be taking place. I think the $25,000-$35,000 advance level for monthly sf lead novels will prove quite viable. In fact at this level good monthly leads, rather than serving as vampires upon a never-lavish sf ad budget, may actually start doing what they are supposed to do, lead the list itself upwards. Further, at least one editor whose list was cut back expressed a certain leavening of satisfaction. He felt that with fewer sf novels coming out each month, he could sell more backlist books.

Backlist books are books that are still in print but are not featured on the monthly order form. A monthly lead is the sf novel that is featured in the monthly solicitation, and the "list" consists of the lead, the new novels, and the reissues of the month. A book stays on the "list" for only a month, but on the order form, all backlist books that are still in print are offered. Best-sellers sell well on the "backlist" for maybe a year, and then they usually evaporate, to be reissued only when the author's next best-seller is published. Science fiction novels, on the other hand. tend to keep selling off the backlist as long as they are kept in print. Trouble is, or has been, that they need to maintain a certain residual level of sales to be kept in print, a level determined by paper and printing costs, warehousing, etc. Publishers without extensive sf experience tend to believe that when monthly sales drop below a certain level the book is on the way out, and it no longer pays to keep it in print. Two thousand copies a month may be an average ballpark figure. When a best-seller dips below that figure, it is indeed for sure dead.

But a science fiction novel that's selling even 100 copies a month will do over 50,000 copies over the term of a five-year contract if it's kept in print and if sales remain stable even at that low level. At 2,000 a month, even a monthly lead will probably sell more copies in five years as a backlist book than it did in its initial distribution.

So the difference between say 1000 copies a month on a backlist book and say 2000 can be very critical. At the lower figure, the book may not be kept in print; at the higher figure it will, and the difference could be as many as 100,000 books over a 5 year contract. Now a difference of 1000 a month is not a lot in absolute terms, so if one less book is published each month and a little more emphasis is put on the backlist, the long-term increase in total sales could be quite disproportionate.

If sf publishing evolves in this direction, it will mean somewhat fewer new books each year, but greater total sales overall. It will also increase the justifiable advances for those books, once publishers are trained to look at the 5-year figures when figuring earn-outs. At this point, $100,000 advances may make a comeback.

But for now, things may be a little tighter on the upper and lower ends of the advance scale. Six figures may be a little harder to obtain, and the competition among newer writers and first novelists may be somewhat stiffer, resulting in a bit of a buyer's market, which may keep obtainable advances for "non-names" a bit below my figure of $10,000. Not that the numbers won't justify a $10,000 advance for almost anything, but the publishers will have a little more leverage in what may no longer quite be a runaway seller's market.

Obviously, it is going to be a little more difficult for an unknown writer to sell a first novel. That's the bad news.

The good news is that it may be becoming a lot easier for a new writer to become known *before* he sells a first novel. The sf book boom has had strange and contradictory effects on the short-fiction market.

As we all know, science fiction has been, for at least a decade, the sole viable habitat of the short story. If you think you've had trouble selling your science fiction stories, try selling any other kind of short fiction. Erotic fiction in men's magazines, one or two detective magazines, the *New Yorker* and a few like it, and after that they pay you in subscriptions. What's more, anything over about 3500 words is generally verboten.

Science fiction, on the other hand, has more viable short-fiction markets that just about everything else put together. In *F&SF, Isaac Asimov's,* and *Analog,* three stable, realiable magazines devoted primarily to fiction, with a total circulation of about 300,000, and a wordage rate in the 4-6¢ a word range. Plus *New Dimensions, Destinies, Universe,* and one-shot books of similar circulation that are also markets for original short fiction, something that is unheard of elsewhere. Plus the shaky latter-day incarnations of *Galaxy, Fantastic,* and *Amazing,* which at least are better than selling your short stories to literary journals which don't even *promise* to pay you. Plus *Galileo* and maybe *UnEarth,* new magazines started from scratch by unknowns.

And then of course there is *Omni,* which is not primarily a science fiction magazine, but which publishes about 15,000 words of sf an issue and pays at close to *Playboy* level, which means near the top for any kind of magazine writing, period.

One would think that this would be the golden age of the science fiction short story, that all these markets would be deluged with good stories, that the level of published sf short fiction would be the highest in history.

But the fact is that the short-fiction markets are *begging* for good short stories. Deluged, the editors are, but with the result of a generation of writers' workshops which have encouraged more people to try to become professional sf writers than ever before. Many of them apparently should not have been encouraged, and during the book boom, those who should have been encouraged were encouraged to concentrate on novels by the availability of book contracts far more lucrative than anything for short fiction.

And, of course, established writers have also been concentrating on books, to the point where most of the recognizable names on book covers are no longer the same names as the names that appear frequently in the contents pages of the magazines.

There's a golden opportunity for some people. The editors are getting great reams of stories, but they are not entranced with the *quality* of the submissions. The old reliable pros, and even the two and three book writers, are concentrating on novels.

By god, if you unpublished and seldom-published writers out there have *good* short fiction to show, you are going to sell it. More than sell it, it's going to be noticed.

Used to be a beginning sf writer had to make a rep for himself in the magazines before getting a novel deal. This was eminently possible if you had the stuff because you were appearing alongside all the greats and near-greats of the field. Possible, not easy. But you certainly did not have to be Mr. Nobody when you tried to get your first book deal. And, of course, if you won an *award* for your short fiction . . .

It's still possible, and a lot easier now. Editors are dying for good short fiction. In the magazines, you're no longer up against so many contributions by the giants of the field.

And some writers have become known via short fiction quite recently—Vonda McIntyre, John Varley, Orson Scott Card, Joan Vinge, to name some obvious examples.

So if the first- and second-novel market gets a little tight, a year or two of concentration on short fiction could bring you your first novel deal with some clout.

Of course there is a catch. The catch is that short-fiction editors are crying for *good* stories, not more submissions. If you ain't got it, you ain't got it, and nothing in this or any other advice column is going to do anything about that.

APRIL 1980
COLUMN 7

What makes science fiction books sell? Of course if we knew the answer to that, we'd all be millionaires, or at least there would be no expensive flops. There's something of a mini panic going on in sf publishing, as the generally putrid state of the national economy as a whole creates the illusion that the great sf bubble may be bursting. Line cutbacks. Uneasy rumors about editors. Tales of six-figure books in the process of bombing. Fewer books being bought. Downward pressure on advances.

Of course in a macroeconomy where the steel industry is halfway to the shitpile and the housing industry is there already, and inflation and interest rates are soaring towards 20%, it would be foolish to suppose that science fiction publishing is going to be immune from the national bummer.

Maybe if sf publishing was still economically marginal, these outside forces would have little or no effect on how many books are bought for $3000 and sell 40,000 copies, but when the advance range is in six figures, and some books have to sell 200,000 copies to be profitable, and big money can be made or lost, and capital has to be invested in books, and therefore has to be borrowed, well, it's the big leagues now, and the prime rate, inflation, and a general economic downturn can affect us.

Which is not to say that publishing in general and science fiction in particular are not in better shape under current economic conditions than most other enterprises. A book which cost three gallons of gas five years ago costs less than two now, paper costs aren't rising as fast as the silver for film or the petroleum for tape and records, and in general, publishing is the least capital-intensive of the entertainment media.

Furthermore, a bleak present means that mass audiences are going to turn away from "realistic" and "mainstream" fiction and towards either nostalgia for unreal golden ages of the past or towards positive visions of a golden hoped-for future.

No, the future for sf in general looks better than the future for the macroeconomy, which is not to say that there won't be certain hard times and difficulties. Indeed, if social conditions push sf publishing into an even more dominant position in popular culture, sf publishing may come more and more to resemble mainstream commercial publishing, in which, it has been said, "There are no more middling books, only hits and flops."

Under these conditions, it is going to be even more necessary than ever to publish science fiction in a cost-effective manner. Which does not simply mean being cheap.

Basically there are now two kinds of sf publishing. The traditional pattern of comparatively small advances, a narrow range of print run and sales, and basically no promotion or advertising, in which books are mass-marketed at minimal cost like widgets, and have little individual visibility. And the new sf publishing, in which large advances are paid, high sales are anticipated and necessary, big money can be made or lost, and one would think major-league advertising and promotion would be in order.

Or so one would think.

But some of the big high-advance books are probably going

to flop and flop badly. Not necessarily because they are turkeys either. The problem is that while there is a laudable tendency towards generosity with advances, there has not, in general, been a realistic assessment about how much advertising and promotion budget you have to put into a $100,000 book to protect your investment. Advance generosity and advertising mingyness is a recipe for disaster.

Effectively advertising a book is not cheap. For one thing, it's a product that's sold nationally, and so only national media are going to be very effective. Previously, there have been two kinds of advertising campaigns for science fiction, when there is any ad budget at all: a fanzine and sf specialty magazine blitz, or a "classy" campaign with a few hyperexpensive ads in places like the NY Times Book Review and Publishers Weekly.

To make any impact using mainstream media, you're talking well north of $25,000 or you're just whistling Dixie. For the same budget, you can really do it up brown in the specialty magazines and fanzines with plenty to spare, but in a certain sense you're just preaching to the faithful.

A publisher who spends much more than $40,000 in advances for an sf novel is going to have to break the novel out of the top end of the genre market to come up smelling of roses instead of a browner substance; and unless that publisher is prepared to throw $25,000 or more into the marketing, he's going to need more luck than a rational person should count on, and really has no business offering such an advance in the first place.

Of course, if a publisher spends $50,000 as an advance on the wrong book—that is a book that cannot benefit from a real ad budget—spending another $25,000 on promotion is just going to be more money down the rathole.

Some books, of course, ultimately succeed by word of mouth, but it takes editorial genius to spot these. Work of genius by either writers or editors is outside the parameters of promotional calculation, and, moreover, literary genius seems, alas, to have no direct relationship to size of advance or to calculating promotability.

But a good many of the big-bucks sf novel sales cannot have been predicated on masterpieces, since in many cases the large advances have been guaranteed for unfinished work. In any kind of rational world, these have to be commercial decisions along the line of "I can sell x number of copies of this book, and I will therefore pay y dollars." Just like the mainstream boys.

Unfortunately, the same calculations do not seem to have

been applied to the other end of the equation in many cases, namely that in order to sell x copies of a book and make it profitable at an advance of y dollars, one must spend z amount on advertising and promotion.

Much above an advance of $30,000, not figuring in an ad budget of at least half the advance is likely to be a bad calculation, at least in the first year or so of publication, upon which editors' track records are unfortunately judged. Anyone who pays a $100,000 advance and doesn't spend $25,000 at bare minumum promoting the book is committing hara kiri, and any writer who takes the money and runs in such a situation may be hurting himself in the long run.

So what is going to have to be learned more thoroughly by writers, science fiction editors, and particularly by the gray eminences who control such things as advertising budgets is, first, how do you cost-effectively market science fiction novels of major importance, and second, how do you pick which novels are to get this treatment? To say that you spend $30,000 promoting novels that have cost you $100,000 is a tautology. The question is, of course, what kind of books have the potential to come out winners in this high-advance, high-advertising, high-visibility framework?

This, of course, is precisely the question that publishers of "best sellers" are always asking themselves.

There seems to be a tendency now to package "important" science fiction novels like mainstream books and try to get "crossover" sales. This, of course, will only work if you are dealing with a crossover novel, one whose theme, setting, and story are easily accessible to other than experienced science fiction readers. If you take a hardcore sf novel, package it as a crossover book, and advertise it in the general national media, it will probably sink like a stone. If you take the same book and the same package and advertise it in the targeted extended sf media, you may get away with it.

If it was me, and I had a fine but hardcore sf novel that I'd paid an "important" advance for, I'd give it a classy but iden-tifiable sf package, and spend most of a $20,000 ad budget in the usual science fiction magazines, *Omni, Starlog, Future, Heavy Metal*, etc., and expect to get out 250,000 copies.

But I would reserve those $100,000 advances for *real* crossover books, on which I would plan to get out house line-leader type numbers, and be willing to spend another $40,000 or so doing it.

So what is a real crossover book? A book that, first of all, is not simplistic to the sophisticated sf market, so that you can spend some of your ad money on a $20,000 targeted sf media campaign, and get out a couple hundred thousand copies to the core sf market. In other words, first and foremost, a good, quality, genuine science fiction novel, not a novelization of a non-existent movie. Secondly, it would be a book that could be picked up and read, at least in theory, by people who had never read a science fiction novel before.

In the real world, what sf novels would have fit these parameters? A few random examples is as far as I'm willing to go in that direction—*The Man in the High Castle, 1984,* Ben Bova's *Colony, A Scanner Darkly, Lucifer's Hammer,* (ahem) *Bug Jack Barron, When Harlie Was One, The Book of Skulls, Behold the Man,* etc., etc., Not space opera, not far-future times or outre planets, not heavy hardware stuff, not exotic action adventure. But not muzak versions of real science fiction novels either.

You will notice that some of these books got the Treatment and made it big, others did not, and some were even commercial flops when published as straight sf or zero-budget mainstream novels *sans* proper advertising and promotion.

You will also notice that many of the "important advance" sf novels of the past couple of years *do not* fit these crossover parameters. Some of them have been promoted as if they did, others have been promoted as sf novels in the targeted media, and some of them have not been adequately promoted at all.

The returns (alas in more senses than one) are now beginning to come in, and it's safe prophecy to say that some of these big books are going to flop badly, others are going to do okay, and a few may justify the investment.

It is not safe prophecy, however, to predict that the publishing industry will draw the right conclusions from the mixed pattern of results that will inevitably occur. One hopes that attention will be paid to what kind of sf, published and promoted how, was successful, and to what kind of judgments made flops— rather than a blanket assumption that sf novels in general do not justify six-figure advances.

As for my predictions on the current crop, I'm not about to play Jimmy the Greek on specific titles, but I'm willing to bet that in general the under-advertised books will do badly, the properly advertised books will do better even when they are not really crossover novels if they are targeted to the sf media, sf novels in misleading mainstream drag will flop if they are hardcore stuff, and properly advertised true crossover novels will do best of all.

OCTOBER 1980
COLUMN 11

Will this be the season that the chickens come home to roost? And whose responsibility are these birds of ill omen anyway? Starting perhaps in the middle of 1980 and running perhaps through the end of 1981, figures will be coming in on the "blockbuster" or more properly "advance limit buster" sf novels sold for big bucks during the peak of the boom. *Titan* in paperback. *Wizard* in boards. The Orson Scott Card novels which raised so much unseemly jealousy among those who thought of themselves as his underpaid betters. *The Snow Queen. Dreamsnake* in paper. *Lord Valentine's Castle. Golem^{100}. Timescape.* Etc. Etc.

One need be neither Cassandra nor Nostradamus to confidently predict that more of them than not will be flops in terms of sales versus advance. One need not be psychic, either, to predict that publishers will try to paint them in red ink to the writers in question even while editors are trying to persuade their corporate masters that the bottom line is really in the black.

It was the misfortune of many of these books, which were bought for big bucks during the peak of a boom, to be published in an el cheapo manner or worse during a period of recession in the macroeconomy and hence a period of lower get-outs and higher returns.

Guess who will be blamed for performances below the expectations expressed in the advances? Gulf+Western? The Ayatollah? Jimmy Carter?

Or the editors who bought them and the writers who wrote them?

It won't be long before novelists who sold books during the boom will be seeking deals for their next books from publishers armed with the sales figures for what these books did during the recession. The art of negotiating being what it is, editors and publishers will surely be trying to use this situation as a bargaining chip in their next round of acquisitions. Writers are going to be told that their big books bombed and therefore, of course, we can't offer you an advance up to your last, but if you're willing to come down considerably, we are still buying a few books here and there....

Now admittedly, even as I intimated at the height of the

feeding frenzy, advances much above $50,000 were not likely to justify themselves in terms of copies sold. At least not based on the first year's get-out. A sale of 150,000 copies is a lot of paperback books, and that is certainly the sort of break-even point editors will be talking about when it comes to justifying another $50,000 advance. Double that for a $100,000 advance and you're talking about a national list paperback seller. And you begin to see that many of our flushest writers may end up in deep shit in contract negotiations to come.

So, since this is a column on economic survival for *writers,* perhaps a kind of reverse evaluation is in order; how well have the science fiction publishers done by the books they have bought?

After all, while the writer is inevitably 100% responsible for the quality of the book, the editor who bought it is 100% reponsible for judging both the literary quality and economic viability of the book. And the writer, unfortunately, has very little indeed to say about what happens to a novel after he returns the proofed galleys. And, sad to say, even the purchasing editor frequently loses control to the corporate powers-that-be after the writer has finished his job and it's time for the publisher to do *its* job.

Selling the book is the publisher's job; perhaps, in the current atmosphere, this elementary fact needs pointing out. The publisher hires the copywriters who write the blurbs and the art directors who commission the covers. The publisher sets the ad budget and buys the space and puts together the copy. The publisher sets the get-out goals for its sales force whose effectiveness partially determines whether they are met. The publisher, not the writer, is responsible for the puissance of the PR department, though of course a writer who is a good and willing public performer is an added asset. Rack space is determined by the strength of the publisher's distribution system. After the writer's work is finished, the fate of the book is in the hands, skillful or otherwise, of this corporate entity.

And so, to varying degrees, is the fate of the editor of the sf line. With the exceptions of DAW and Del Rey, imprints run by the names in question, most sf editors do not occupy chairs of publishing control. In many cases, the sf editors must deal with an art director who does the publisher's whole line, who is a power at least as strong as he is within the house, and whose good will must be maintained by compromise, or worse. The sf editor's ad budget—if he has one—is set by a power structure in place above him. The sales force must sell *all* the house's books, and so operates along its own imperatives, not necessarily those of the sf line. And distributors speak only to God.

In cold reality, the sales performance of a novel depends at least as much on corporate follow-through as it does on either the literary quality of the work or the editorial acumen of the acquiring editor. Of course, corporations being corporations, the bad karma of corporate failures will be dumped on the editor; and, humans being humans, the editor, in turn, will try to pass as much of it as possible on to the writer.

If writers evaluated sf publishers the way publishers evaluate writers, how would *they* look in terms of track record?

In general, not too swift.

The case of *Lord Valentine's Castle* has been detailed in these pages. Had Harper & Row spent the $35,000 they had guaranteed as an ad budget with any degree of intelligence, this $127,000 book might have done 30,000 in boards, which would have caused Bantam to protect its $75,000 investment with an ad campaign of similar proportion, and the whole thing might well have been profitable for all concerned. But Harper "forgot" to spend the money until it was too late to be cost-effective.

Now most people, including yours truly, put this down to sheer incompetence, albeit in a Guiness record class. But one well-known paranoiac suggested that they forgot deliberately because they *wanted* the book to fail. "Burying their mistakes," he said dourly. "They do it all the time."

Writing off a $125,000 investment?

It seemed improbable, until someone told me that six out of ten monthly *line-leaders,* the great big six-figure mainstream would-be best sellers, *flop* at a very successful major paperback house, and this is not unusual for the industry, which makes a profit off a success rate of 40%!

Somehow, Toto, I don't think we're in Kansas.

True, very few sf novels are in this economic class, which I would call the "A" novels, far too few for their various fates to be extrapolated into a curve for the industry as a whole. The majority of sf novels published annually are "C" novels—non-lead books bought for small advances, with no advertising or promotion, small expectations, and the sales to match the results of this self-fulfilling prophecy. Not so long ago, almost all sf novels were "C" novels, and it was virtually impossible for them to succeed or fail individually; the karma of the line was the karma of the book. This kind of publishing will always be modestly profitable for the publisher and a hardscrabble existence for the writers.

And this, unfortunately, seems in many cases to be the corporate perception of sf publishing, even after laying out big bucks in advances.

In between the *sui generis* "blockbuster" "A" novels and the proletarian "C" books is the true heart of the transformation in sf publishing, the "B" books, science fiction's emerging affluent middle class.

I'm talking about paperback monthly leaders, sometimes done as originals, sometimes bought at auction from hardcover houses, sometimes generated by the line's own hardcover imprint, *a la* Pocket Books, Berkley, and Del Rey. Books of some significance, no more than twelve a year per house, with acquisition costs in the $25,000 to $50,000 range. This phenomenon is as new as the blockbusters and it represents the mainstream of the new economics of sf publishing. It's what has enabled a sizeable collective of sf writers to live like human beings for the first time. It's not a crapshoot like the blockbusters. Competently published, most of the "B" books should be profitable in this advance range.

What does "properly published" mean in this context? By the numbers, published in such a way as to distribute about 150,000 paperbacks, and sell about 90,000, a return rate of 40%. This will earn out a $20,000 advance in the first year, and will make a $35,000 advance quite profitable for the publisher. Add a hardcover that gets out 15,000 copies and sells 10,000, and a $50,000 advance pans out gold.

Now this is not minimal "C" novel publishing. It requires skilled packaging, a motivated sales force, the proper ad budget, and a clear perception of sales goals on the part of the publisher.

One would think that this would all be worked out logically based on the consistent advance range for this kind of book. If you know your profit point is 90,000 copies, then you do what it takes to sell 90,000 copies. You package the book as something befitting this expectation. You put $10,000 to $20,000 in a well-targeted ad campaign, and by a trade ad campaign you let distributors, bookstores, and your own salesmen know you are backing the product in a businesslike way.

Is this the way these backbones of the industry are being published?

One hot rumor in the Big Apple is that the president of a certain major paperback house—a house which has been buying heavily in this "B" novel market—is of the opinion that sf is "penny ante" stuff. The house that pioneered the hardcover-softcover deal which is most beneficial to publishers in this market has cut back its hardcover list.

And at another major paperback house, the corporate god has potentially torpedoed the new sf hardcover line designed to feed these middle-cost line leaders into the paperback line by declaring that the ad budget for six significant hardcovers shall be zero.

The logic seems to be that if these books don't sell their 100,000 copies, it's the fault of the editor and the writer, not of the ignorant art director who packaged a "B" book like a "C" book, nor of the accountant who killed the ad budget, nor of the promotion department that was out to lunch.

If the publishing industry were an auto company it would be Chrysler.

Somehow, the perception carried over from previous decades that sf was automatic publishing; that the books sold what they would sell without any real support. Therefore, if you pay a larger advance, you will somehow get larger sales without having to back up the product.

This from an industry with a *line-leader* flop rate of over 50%!

Pity the poor sf editor. He buys books he believes in as leads in the expectation they will get the support they warrant and pays the going rate for same accordingly. If that support is not forthcoming and the books do not live up to the expectations set by the advance, he must play the heavy with his writers, whose confidence is his stock in trade, and use a corporate failure as an excuse to bargain down the price on the next one. Otherwise his ass is grass.

I have more than once pointed out that the publishing industry is being gobbled up by entertainment conglomerates. Now we begin to see the results. In the TV game, better than 90% of all projected series are expensive flops. For Paramount or MCA, the remaining 10% generate the profits. We are now dealing with the same corporations, hence the same corporate mentality. Expectation of a high rate of failure. Unwillingness therefore to invest the energy and money necessary to make each book count. A revolving door for production executives and editors based on the Nielsens, on the sacred Bottom Line.

From time to time, one hears moans about the disloyalty of writers, how the SOBs will leave one publisher for another for a lousy few grand in increased advances, how writers no longer take the long view, failing to realize that proper and consistent publishing with the same house is what builds the value of a writer's total *ouvre* in the long run.

Indeed, in the boom times, there has been some justice in this complaint. Where now will be the publishers' loyalty to their writers in this leaner time? Indeed, where will be the publishers' corporate loyalty to their own editors?

It looks like there'll be some hard bargaining in the months to come. Many writers will have unpleasant figures waved in their faces and be asked to take lower advances because their previous novels were balance sheet failures. What possible answer can there be to this?

Well, writers might screw up their courage and inquire as to who really didn't live up to the previous bargain—themselves, whose work was appraised before a dime was invested, or their corporate lessee, who failed to properly market the property they had knowingly invested in? What happened to the package? What happened to the ad budget? Why was it considered sound business to pay out a large advance and turn into Uncle Scrooge when it was time to back it up?

Loyalty? What greater act of faith than for a writer to sell another book to a house that—perhaps due to economic hard times or a temporary fit of corporate incompetence—screwed up the previous one according to its own definition of failure? With only a modest inflation escalator in the advance, of course.

Pity the poor sf editor, caught between his writers on one hand, whose confidence he can hardly maintain while trying to cut their wage, and the corporate mavens who failed to support his line in the manner which his advance range should have assured. Either way, he's the fall guy.

JUNE 1981
COLUMN 12

It has been admittedly many a moon since this column last appeared, a season during which I experienced what it is like to be an sf writer media event in France, wrote a new science fiction novel not entirely in English called *The Void Captain's Tale*, served as President of SFWA, and had my first record released. All this is not so much in the way of news or boast (I'll do a better job at some point in the *People* column) but to explain that while I realize that this column is my main *raison d'etre* (I keep meeting people who've read nothing else I've written), $40 a pop does not pay the rent, and even I find it necessary from time to time to take my own advice and moonlight as something other than a *Locus* columnist.

Also, truth be told, about the time my last column appeared, I was coming to think that maybe I had said it all, or at any rate all I had to say, and that if I kept going just for the sake of appearing in *Locus* every month, I might start degenerating into repetitious babble.

However, just as many things have transpired in my own career since my last column, so, too, has the Great Wheel done a few turns in sf at large, not to mention the greater body politic, and it behooves all survival-minded old dogs and young pups to take a look at the tricks of their trade in light of the current karma.

On the publishing slot front, there is good news and bad news. The good news is that Jim Baen and Tom Dougherty are publishing their first Tor Books, Holt is inching into the field as a hardcover publisher as witness their publication of the next Nebula volume, Ace Books is going to ten sf novels a month, and Terry Carr is reviving the old Ace SF Specials on a separate list of six per annum.

There, that didn't take very long, did it?

As for the bad news....

Doubleday is cutting its sf list in half, and the half they are dropping are essentially the books the corporate powers-that-be consider "non-juvenile." Berkley/Putnam is eliminating their regular sf hardcover line and will only do sf superstars in boards from here on in. Simon & Schuster in its Timescape incarnation will do six sf hardcovers a year instead of twelve. And the entire Dell/Quantum sf program has been shitcanned after the usual annual putsch in higher circles, along with its major domo, Jim Frenkel.

You don't need me to tell you that good news this ain't. But what it all means may not be as obvious as it seems on the surface.

Obviously it means that there has been a severe contraction in sf publishing. Or does it? As far as paperback goes, it doesn't. The loss of an entire sf program at a major publisher cloaks the fact that Ace is increasing its schedule, a new publisher born of sf is starting up from scratch, and one of the great (yes, Terry, great) book editors of the golden age of same is returning to the lists with idealistic intent. When you consider that Timescape, DAW, Del Rey, et al., are holding steady, you are probably looking at an *increase* in total slots for paperback sf books.

The collapse, it would appear, is confined to *hardcover* sf, and even here things are a little deceptive. The Doubleday hardcover line—in terms of advances, sales expectations, etc.—is a throwback to the days when their heavy competition for the boot work by the best writers was Gnome Press, and despite the major league stature of the company, the line has for a long time been essentially a bottom market. The Simon & Schuster sf line was starving to death for total lack of advertising money book by book at twelve a year and the contraction to six as Timescape may make them a first-line hardcover publisher of sf in execution as well as name.

A writer of my acquaintance has even opined that with fewer sf hardcovers being published, those that are published will do better, because the market had become glutted.

Still, there is no denying that the Dell program is dead, less hardcovers are being published, and in the loss of Berkley/Putnam as a hardcover line, one of sf's flagships has reduced itself to secondary status.

Do you get the feeling that the inner meaning of the shift is still somewhat elusive? That an element is missing from this discourse, the same element that seems to have lately disappeared from discussions of "the state of the industry"? Dare I say it? I do believe, I finally do.

Quality.

According to one editor, the books that *that worthy* considers quality at the sf line are not moving, whereas the self-admitted commercial crap bought by same is. One of the field's most innovative novelists has been forced onto welfare. And then there are this year's nominations for the Hugos in the novel category.

Charlie Brown, in his diplomatic journalese, contented himself in these pages with an exhaustive exegesis of the facts, but this is forthrightly a column of opinion, and one written by someone, moreover, who was a working critic during the period of these nominees' publication; and for what it is worth, my opinion is that this year's Hugo nominations are not only an unprecedented disgrace to the honor of science fiction but one of an insidiously pernicious species.

No less than three out of five nominees are sequels to previously proven products. Of the other two, one received the highest advance in the history of the field at the time, and the other still probably holds the record for ad budget. The Nebula winner, *Timescape*, failed to make the Hugo ballot for the first time in history. Another sf editor has privately opined that only one of the Hugo nominees might possibly be said to have true literary ambition, and even this, we were able to agree, is a borderline case.

Notice that I have been able to state the case, whether you agree or not, without having to deal specifically with what exists between the covers of these five Hugo nominees. The business details describe the situation.

And that is exactly the horrid point.

Cinema, you will note, has devolved in the direction of prime time television, with the movie series. Prime time TV has devolved in the direction of soaps via serials like *Dallas* and *Hill Street Blues*. Politics has devolved into a mediocre B movie. And the decline we subliminally sense in sf is part of this devolutionary trend, which, in the final analysis, seems to be a devolution in the general quality of public consciousness.

Quality. Perhaps in these dim days it is necessary to strictly define this term.

As one who has listened to the palaver of both publishing executives and Hollywood wheeler-dealers and watched the two species converge, I can define quality negatively as that which is absent as a factor from the current commercial decisions of same, or at least absent as a factor from the cybernetic decisions made by the entertainment conglomerates whom they now by and large both serve. The bottom line is now as much the bottom line in publishing as it is in Hollywood. The only relevant questions now are what can we gross with what kind of package and how much do we put into hype? Once these figures are set, the fate of a book or a movie is pretty much sealed. Package and budget become both self-fulfilling prophecy and literary definition.

During the ascending period of the boom, sf remained to a large extent in an earlier time zone in relationship to the general corporate devolution of cultural product. As long as advertising and hype for sf novels remained roughly equal—at a pittance level—that illusive thing called quality has some causal effect on sales and awards. Reviews and word-of-mouth being the principal vectors of communication, what was inside the covers of the package tended to dominate its destiny, though the covers themselves set the limits on what success sf in general might achieve.

But as advances climbed at the top end and in general started to vary almost as much as advances in publishing in general, ad budgets began to appear and become important, and convention hype began to draw the attention of sf publishers. Finally, we achieved the ultima thule of a contract for a major sf novel including escalator clauses setting dollar value on performance in the Hugo and Nebula competitions.

Somewhere along the line, the corporate power structures began overlaying their vibes on our little pocket universe.

Doubleday's rationale for halving their sf list, *their own public explanation,* mind you, was in effect that the PG books were marginally successful on the juvenile market, but the Rs, what they publicly called the "adult sf novels," had Nielsens sufficiently crappy to be shitcanned. The entire Dell line was canceled as a byproduct of corporate reshuffling. Sf boomed far enough into the big time to finally draw the attention of the cost-accountant mavens who dominate publishing.

Welcome to the land of the Sacred Bottom Line.

Now that we know where we are, we can begin to understand where we have arrived at. Just as the episodic series has long dominated television and more recently has become box office at the movies, so does this non-esthetic now come to invade our literary realm. Hardly surprising, since both tentacles of the cultural manufactories now lead back to the same entertainment octopus.

The esthetic of the episodic series is absolute and unitary: the Nielsens, or their literary equivalent. An episodic series format (I've worked on a few) is designed towards one end—to attract as large an audience as possible for each episode, and to keep the series going as long as possible. A consistent and comfortable alternate reality that the audience can slip into week after week or book after book is essential, and there must be no unseemly intrusions of larger forces into its Disneyland confines. One must have one or more continuous characters with whom the audience identifies who can undergo no personality changes lest that hopefully time-worn identification weaken a few rating points. Each book or episode in the series must be more like every other episode than it is like itself or the thing will have the whiff of the "anthology series" about it, which as we all know is rating poison.

A work of art (first "Quality," and now fucking *"Art!"*) on the other hand, has its own self-contained structure with a pleasing internal resolution, and at its highest form, the science fiction novel, is most often the tale of transformation in reality, character, or both—exactly that sublime thematic element excluded as *seppuku* from the successful series guide.

And that, in a nutshell, is why "quality" is excluded as a parameter in discussions of the state of the industry, why the

Hugo ballot for novel is what it is, and why writers who have yet to sell their first novels are already planning series.

It is also the missing piece of the puzzle of what is really happening to the sf industry, the unexamined center, the explanatory void.

Jim Frenkel, whatever his strengths and weaknesses, was dedicated to the principle that certain books should be published on their own terms rather than as interchangeable monthly product. Exit Jim Frenkel and his sf line. Interesting to note that rumor hath it that Dell will start over on some other basis once the dust of its latest in a long series of exits from the field has cleared. Interesting to note, too, that Putnam will continue to do the Herberts and the Heinleins in boards, leaving the Berkley paperback line to the less exalted. Even more interesting in a ghastly way is the fact that Simon & Schuster hocked every line in their operation to buy an unwritten first sf novel by Carl Sagan for $2 million, a sum that would have left Timescape Books, on whose list this sf novel will *not* appear, flush for half a decade.

Prime time TV, after all, also has a class structure. There are the bread-and-butter episodic series, and then there are the big blockbuster mini-series. The occasional superstar turn gets superstar exposure and budget, and everything else is run on a cost-accounting basis.

It is perhaps best to cliff-hang *this* episode with a thought or two about Timescape Books as a phenomenon, since the current reshuffle puts its editor, David Hartwell, in the catbird seat of more editorial power than any single editor of books has ever before had in the sf genre. Timescape is now the only sf publisher who can consistently offer selected writers a combined hard-cover/paperback deal. This means that, first, Timescape will have first crack at the cream of the field, and, second, the other paperback sf publishers will either have to involve themselves in auctions for the fewer remaining hot hardcover properties or lead their lines with paperback originals.

On the other hand, Timescape, in its previous double incarnation, had a line ad budget of zilch for the strongest line of books in the genre. When the transmogrification was made, it was hoped in various quarters that this was a new harbinger of looser purse strings on the ad side, as witness the big spread in *Publisher's Weekly*. Now that S&S is in hock up to its eyeballs for Carl Sagan's unwritten first sf novel, a deal concocted in more exalted corporate realms, one wonders whether that infusion of green corpuscles will indeed be forthcoming.

Make no mistake about it, the karma of the situation is that in pragmatic terms, Timescape Books has emerged as sf's flagship publisher. It cannot but attract the heavies, and it has four or five slots a month to develop the heavies of the near future. It is also up to its ears in submissions.

No sf line has ever been in a better competitive position. How it fares in the greater context will mirror the fortunes of the sf genre in general. And perhaps the spirit as well.

AUGUST 1981
COLUMN 13

Having in the last exciting episode at last brought the illusive question of quality into our discussion of the dialectic between the science fiction writer and the commercial interface, it now behooves us to hold our noses and attempt to examine the effect of current corporate thinking in the sf industry upon the esthetic state of the art. And, since this *is* still a column about survival as a science fiction writer, what this means to the writer as both an artist and a businessman. Let's face it, even the most cynical hack began writing sf out of idealistic intent, or he would have chosen a less demanding and more lucrative literary venture such as TV script writing, and even those of us of the most ivory-tower purity have to pay the rent.

Last time out, I pointed to Timescape Books as having emerged from the latest round of shifts as the flagship publisher of the sf genre, and the sf line in the best current competitive position. Charlie Brown suggested to me when he read that column that perhaps it painted too rosy a picture of the karma of a house that just happened to be my main publisher.

But in this case, I wasn't just praising the editorial acumen of David Hartwell (who has had the wisdom to buy several of my novels), I was pointing to the catbird seat that Timescape Books now finds itself in in a purely commercial sense.

Aside from Del Rey, Timescape is the only remaining sf line to offer a hardcover/paperback combined deal. And despite Berkley's corporate stupidity in dropping its hardcover line, this remains the best way to publish science fiction.

Large statement? Look at the numbers:

In a combined hardcover/paperback deal, the writer gets 100% of the royalties on both hardcover and paper, instead of splitting the paperback royalties with the hardcover publisher. That's what makes such a capacity on the part of an sf publisher such a competitive edge in seeking monthly line-leaders.

From the publisher's point of view, such a deal means that instead of involving himself in feeding-frenzy auctions for paperback leaders, he can develop these books himself with his hardcover line. And from the hardback viewpoint, it becomes cost-effective to advertise your sf novels because what you're enhancing is the value of something your company already owns, namely the paperback rights.

Thus, done right, this publishing strategy means more books sold at less initial outlay, and what the writer gets out of it may be less advance for the paperback rights in theory, but 100% of the royalties on all sales. This makes such synergetic sense that a cynic might wonder how the sf industry was able to invent it.

And, of course, one should never underestimate the ability of the current corporate mentality to fuck a good thing up.

This kind of deal is relatively new. The accounting procedures have yet to catch up. Berkley, you have heard, has just decided to drop this kind of publishing. How could they do such a stupid thing, you may ask?

Trouble is, even at publishing corporations which own both paperback and hardcover operations, the books are kept separately. Richard Snyder, maven of Simon & Schuster, unilaterally axed the ad budget for the S&S hardcover sf line to zero because from the point of view of Simon & Schuster, whose balance sheet is his own personal Nielsen, advertising sf novels was not cost-effecitve. True, putting some push behind the hardcovers would greatly enhance the paperback sales, but that would redound to the black ink credit of *Pocket Books.* Moreover, S&S would not get any paperback auction money, and hardcover publishers live at least as much by copping half the paperback money as by selling their own books. So from this point of view, spending $20,000 in ad money to push the sales of an sf novel from 5,000 to 20,000 copies does not appear cost-effective on the hardcover budget.

When you look at hardcover sales of sf novels alone under these circumstances, which is to say the sales of books that are published with no push, you come to the same conclusion that Doubleday has, namely that publishing sf in hardcover is not a profitable proposition. And if you are Berkley, you foolishly decide to drop your hardcover sf line.

If you are Pocket Books, however, you seem to have taken a different tack. Someone there, whether David Hartwell, or Ron Busch, or some other gray eminence, seems to have realized that the true purpose of an sf hardcover line is to feed line-leaders to the paperback line. Because when you account both editions together, you come up a winner.

Thus, apparently, Timescape Books is essentially a Pocket Books operation, whose hardcovers are in effect *Pocket Books* hardcovers, just as the Del Rey sf hardcovers are *Ballantine* books.

And that is why, with the demise of the Dell program and the exit of Berkley from publishing a hardcover sf line, Timescape and Del Rey are left as the publishers of sf with the most competitive set-ups. And Del Rey in a certain sense chooses not to compete for the full spectrum of science fiction, operating off a rather precise technical definition of what fits into their market as they perceive it and how much they are willing to pay for same.

At the same time, you will note, the transmogrification of the Pocket/S&S line into Timescape Books completes a process that has been quietly proceeding for some time. Namely that sf is now published by the major full-spectrum paperback houses under, in effect, separate brand names. DAW, as its own logo proclaims, =SF. Del Rey, of course, is the brand name of Ballantine sf. Berkley and Bantam have developed their own sf logos, and Dell, before its demise, operated under both Dell SF and Quantum imprints. And now we have Timescape Books.

Timescape, it is interesting to note, spent more money advertising its new brand name than was ever spent on an entire year's line of Pocket or S&S science fiction. Indeed, more money was spent on the design of the Timescape logo than on any book in the line, including its namesake.

By which route we have arrived at the whole unsavory question of "sf packaging."

Quite obviously sticking a separate brand name on the sf line, let alone springing for big bucks to design a logo, is strictly a packaging decision, and one of considerable import. And it is here that the question of quality interfaces with commercial considerations with a vengeance.

Time out of mind, sf writers have complained about the sleazy packaging of their books. Time out of mind, have publishers, at least among themselves, countered with the perception that the traditional sleazy packaging successfully reaches the intended market. And, indeed, if the visual buttons of the sf readership are located by sf packagers through a perusal of fanzines, convention art shows, and the sartorial splendors of con-going fandom, it is not hard to see where this perception comes from.

And, of course, decades of consistent packaging, whatever the quality, becomes a self-fulfilling prophecy—by now, everyone knows what sf looks like on the meatrack.

During the ascending boom, advances got bigger and publishing aspirations got higher, but the packaging really did not change to meet the altered perception of the targeted market. Partly this was because sf has always gotten short shrift from art directors.

Art directors are usually responsible for the covers of every book in the line, and sf, therefore, looms not large in their consciousness. Since art directors are responsible for the covers of all editors' books at a house, they generally have more clout than any one editor, certainly more than the sf editor, and most editors live in fear of attracting their ire. Thus, most sf packaging is concocted by people with little interest in sf, often less knowledge, and frequently no little measure of contempt.

From this point of view, a science fiction novel is just one more slice of sf, to be packaged not according to its own idiosyncratic nature, but according to the standard sf parameters. Notice, for example, that Timescape and previous Pocket sf packages for the most part have their titles and authors' names lettered in standard faces, whereas many other Pocket Books have carefully designed custom lettering jobs integrated with the illo.

Pre-boom, with more or less standard advances, standard print runs, and standard sales expectations for sf, this made a kind of ruthless commercial sense. But one of the reasons that the boom has declined has been the disappointing performance of high-advance sf novels when it comes to breaking out of the standard sales parameters. And one of the reasons for this has been the fact that many of these books were still packaged with the same indifference as the rest of the sf. And marketed likewise.

Now, with the whole publishing industry in recession and horns being pulled in, we have the ascendancy of distinctive line packaging of sf, rather than the individual packaging of sf novels. Minimalist sf publishing is making a comeback.

This may turn out to be the true lesson of the firing of Jim Frenkel. Rumor hath it that after Dell has wormed out of paying acceptance money on all the high-ticket items of sf that would be coming in under contract, they will re-enter the genre with a new editor dedicated to reduced expenditures and reduced expectations.

Back up go the ghetto walls at a higher economic level but with a reinforced rigor. Now we will not merely have consistently sleazy packaging of sf which discourages all but the hardened aficionado, we will have this mentality officially enshrined in the segregation of sf from the rest of major houses' lines by separate logos or even pulp pseudonyms.

But wait a minute.

Is not *God Emperor of Dune* serenely ensconced in the higher reaches of the national trade best-seller list? Was there ever a more self-proclamatory sf title? Has not Carl Sagan been forthrightly paid $2 million for what is described as an unwritten first science fiction novel? Are not new novels by Farmer and LeGuin reviewed in *Time*? Is Benford's *Timescape* not published in paper *without* the Timescape logo?

Berkley, you will note, while canceling its regular hardcover sf line, announced that they will continue to publish the Herberts and Heinleins and Farmers in hardcover. Stupid enough to throw away another *God Emperor of Dune*, they are not! Timescape Books will *not* have its imprint on the Sagan sf novel, nor was *Timescape* a Timescape Book.

In other words, science fiction novels that are obvious bets to transcend the genre sales parameters *will* be called science fiction novels on occasion, but they will be removed from the science fiction line.

What this means for the lucky few is that it is possible to have a science fiction novel published as such in a first-class manner. What it means for everyone else whose book is published within the packaging of an sf line is that expectations must have a rigidly-defined ceiling.

Packaging strategies tell the story. The first incarnation of the Timescape logo was a huge one-inch banner smeared across the top of every book like the Kellogg's ensign. About as prideful to the author of what was inside as being forced to wear a yellow Star of David. This was later shrunk to something slightly less offensive. The August titles shrink the logo much farther but add consistent line layout and design which over-rides the illos and titles and forces everything into a consistent line package in the manner of the late, lamented Laser.

Whatever the individual design, this packaging strategy openly proclaims that the identity of the line is deemed of more importance than the individual identities of the books published under its aegis.

Which is why sf novels which clearly *must* have individual

packaging identity, such as *God Emperor of Dune, Timescape* itself, or the Sagan book, *cannot* rationally be published in such packages, which means that they cannot be published within sf lines.

What, you may ask, does all this have to do with quality?

What indeed? How possible will it be for sf writers to dedicate themselves to producing works of the highest quality of which they are capable, at the full stretch of their talents, when they *know* that a contract with an sf line means second-class publishing before a word is even writen?

Of course there have always been the righteous and lonely heroes of sf—the Phil Dicks and the Brian Aldisses—who have maintained their dedication to the best that is within them in the face of this situation. Perhaps there always will be.

But now, in addition to this ancient fate of the sf writer, there is the possible dream of a way out. For the supremely talented, or the lucky, or the well-connected, or those with the cynical craftsmanship necessary to adapt the sf novel to the best-seller level of popular writing, there is the possibility of having one's science fiction novel published as such but outside the limits of regular sf lines.

Thus, under these circumstances, an sf logo itself is in danger of becoming an open admission of second-class citizenship even within the literary realm of science fiction itself. And since, by the nature of things, there will be room in the marketplace for only a handful of "mainstream sf novels" in any year, many worthy sf novels will sink into the slimy green ichor without a trace. And those who write them will know up front that this will be their most likely fate.

How much easier, how much less painful to the spirit, to sell a science fiction adventure series, further from the heart and less taxing to the book-by-book imagination, more lucrative and more pleasing to our corporate masters, than that which is conceived as a segment of life's work in manic dedication.

PART THREE
CONS, AWARDS, AND THE CON CON

The literature of science fiction has, for about half a century, had a national, indeed world-wide, subculture structured around it known as "science fiction fandom." For almost as long, these highly-organized fans have been holding weekend-long bashes called "science fiction conventions," the social, and to an extent, commercial centers of the sf world. These days, a determined and well-heeled debauchee can attend a "con" somewhere just about every week of the year, and during the high season, say from March through October, will have to choose which of several to attend.

The largest and most important of these events is the World Science Fiction Convention or "Worldcon," held annually at the end of summer in a city chosen by competitive bidding at a previous Worldcon. It is the attendees, or more precisely, paid-up members, of the Worldcon who vote for the annual Hugo Awards in various categories—best sf novel, best short story, best dramatic presentation, best editor, best artist, etc.

Since 1965, the Science Fiction Writers of America have awarded the Nebulas, given away at the annual Nebula Awards Banquet.

These and other awards in the genre are described in some detail and even rated in this section. Alas, some sad updating is required. The Prometheus Award no longer exists. Also, more significantly, the American Book Award is no longer awarded in the category of science fiction.

After the first TABAs, elements of the New York Literary

Establishment, still smarting from the pain of having the National Book Awards, which they had controlled, transmogrified into the American Book Awards, which were much more broadly based, staged a partially successful counter-coup. Led by the mavens of PEN among others, the NYLE continued to heap abuse on TABA, threatened boytott, and even set up a PEN award which they touted as the new NBA.

The NYLE no longer has the power in the publishing industry it once had; the bottom line has thus far prevailed, TABA has not been slain, nor has the NYLE gained control of the judging. But they did still have enough clout left to exert sufficient pressure to gain a concession from the real publishing powers that be. The number of awards categories were cut; among the axed awards were those for science fiction.

"Science fiction," it was said, "has its own awards." That is a fact which certainly cannot be denied. And in a way the "mainstream" has its own fandom, replete with insular power-cliques, behavior codes, and fanzine feuds. As well as permanent controversy over awards.

In fact, the NYLE just held its first con in 1981 at the Roosevelt Hotel in New York. $25 for advance registration, $50 at the door. Three thousand mainstream writing groupies and would-be writers attended panels featuring big-name pros. There was the beginning of a primitive huckster room. No masquerade, no art show, no free con parties in the con suite.

The "Con Committee" was The Nation Foundation, and, as sometimes happens, there was a certain controversy about the proceeds. The NYLE con was about the size of a small Worldcon, charged a similar admission, and, as sf fans know, you can run such a con at a small profit—especially if you don't run a masquerade or an art show or a film program or a con suite.

But if sf fans could teach the NYLE something about putting on a con, and they certainly can, the NYLE could teach sf fans something about another sort of con. You see, various publishers kicked in contributions to this event to the tune of $150,000! On top of that, the Nation Foundation claimed they lost $30,000 in the bargain! And when asked if they would publish the figures in a final con report, they declared that since they were a non-profit organization, they were not legally required to do so.

Science fiction has its own awards.

And now the NYLE has its own con.

Anyone for Switzerland in 1984?

JANUARY 1980
COLUMN 4

Well, that time of year is rolling around again, the annual sf awards frenzy, which begins as SFWA closes recommendations for the Nebula at the turn of the year and doesn't really stop till the Hugos are awarded at the Worldcon at summer's end. Since about 1965 the Hugo and the Nebula have been regarded as the two major awards in the field, but they are no longer alone, and this year they even have some heavyweight competition.

So while we're all praying and scrambling to be awarded the something for best something of the year, it seems like a good idea to turn things around a little bit, and look over the nominations for best science fiction award of 1980.

The good old Hugo award has to be a favored contender. It's the old pro in the field and has to be ahead this year as always on sentiment alone. It has the largest demographic base, and since it is awarded at the biggest awards party, it has high visibility and good vibes with the movers and shapers on the party circuit. On the other hand, it must be admitted that it is a straight popularity contest among hardcore fans and does not necessarily represent even popularity among a really representative readership, in terms of the total sf audience. As for measured critical judgment....

We have the Nebula awards, given by the writers to their peers. Or at least that's what they're supposed to be, a sophisticated guild judgment by fellow craftsmen. What stands in the way of realization of this award's high artistic aspiration is the nuts and bolts of plotting out the process, though it must be admitted that the work is rich in sub-plots. The rules change from year to year and sometimes from moment to moment, and the reality depicted is satisfyingly ambiguous. Though nothing that has won a Nebula has been totally off the wall, and no smelly scandal has ever surfaced, and something like 40% of the 500 members do vote (which is certainly at least par for your average writers' organization), the mystique exists that Something is Wrong, though no one seems to know what it is. With 500 writers involved, you're not going to get a linear, clear-cut award but one fraught with new-wave ambivalences and a certain Van Vogtian complication. Maybe not this year, but coming up fast.

Sure to be an instant favorite with new-wave nihilists and cynical hacks alike is the Prometheus award. True, it is given away by a small committee associated with the Libertarian Party for a work best expressing the principles of that group and might therefore be regarded as something of a small press oddity. But there's nothing small about the magnanimity of the trophy. Not some rocks set in lucite or a mingy scroll or even a shiny aluminum rocket ship, the Prometheus Award consists of $2500 in gold. Now that's what I call putting your money where your mouth is. You can argue about whether a Hugo or Nebula is worth something on a book cover, but the Prometheus has concrete value even to the gnomes of far-off Zurich! Since every writer who needs money will have a soft spot in his heart for this ringing prose, the Prometheus has to be a hot contender for best science fiction award of the year. You leave the theater humming the tune.

The John W. Campbell Award for best novel of the year (not the quasi-Hugo for best new writer) is a perfect example of an academic anthology. Its heart is in the right place, and it comes up with interesting and provocative choices, but typos are rife, and the paperwork is screwed up. It's hard to figure out where the committee comes from. I remember seeing Campbell's name misspelled on a glossy poster turned out for the event, and the reception consisted of a pay bar in a basement rec room. Needs another draft.

The Jupiter Award is given out by an organization of college and high school sf teachers, but where, and when, I have never been able to fathom. I got a scroll once for finishing second, but when I won the thing, I learned about it in *Locus*. Good idea, but this one reads like an outline for an award rather than a finished novel. Needs to be fleshed out before it can be considered a contender.

Despite its inherent limitations, the Locus Award gets more credible every year. Now it is awarded at the Westercon, and maybe soon Charlie will spring for a statue. Send in your designs! I vote for a gold-plated computerized typewriter. After all, Charlie, almost as many people vote for it as vote for the Hugo, and you have an awards banquet already....Could be a comer.

The Prix Apollo is exotic, imported Fench stuff, given by a jury of official worthies to the best science fiction novel published in France that year by foreigner or native. So stringent are their criteria that the local stuff hardly ever wins; it obviously takes a serious-minded group of idealists to tell their fellow countrymen that they don't make it. No free trip to Paris layed on, a flaw that if corrected could give the Prix Apollo a breakthrough on the American market. Meantime, an insouciant little award in the Old World style, more likely to appeal to connoisseurs than to the mass American audience.

Ah, but now we come to a brand new award, the first science fiction award to attempt to bridge the gap between sf and mainstream, the American Book Award for best hardcover and best paperback science fiction novel. This one really has a crossover plot-line which may give it appeal to science fiction award fans and mainstream award readers alike.

The American Book Awards are more or less given by the total publishing industry itself. Used to be they were the National Book Awards, and there was only one for fiction in all categories. Great turmoil gripped the New York Literary Establishment at the democratization of these awards, not by writers and editors, but by the publishing mavens. It was a pretty good fanzine feud for a while.

The American Book Awards for sf will be chosen by a fairly complex jury system involving writers, publishers, critics, librarians, and editors, chosen from among volunteers. Since this awards ceremony will be the publishing industry's attempt at its maximum media bash, and since the publishing industry itself has a stake in the credibility of the American Book Awards, they will certainly have credibility when it comes to negotiating a major motion picture, and it may make it. Science fiction awards join mainstream!

Of course, the American Book Awards also have a certain appeal for genre awards enthusiasts too, with their Nebula-like plot-line, and their shadowy jury system, reminiscent of the Jupiter, and the Campbell, and the Apollo.

Could turn out to be the best science fiction award of the year, if not in 1980, then later. A shoo-in for the International Fantasy Award Memorial Award for best new science fiction award of the year.

And there you have the contenders for the best science fiction award of the year, a bumper crop to ring in the 1980s.

Now what does all this have to do with stayin' alive? Well that is very much the question. How important are these awards to the career of a science fiction writer? Which ones? Do you campaign for them? How? Is it possble? Is it moral? What does this stuff do to your head?

It is difficult to see how any award can have a negative impact on your income. You can put "Something Award Winner" on all your books forevermore and it's certainly not going to scare any customers away. Some might argue that it's not going to attract any either, but there's no way of telling.

It should be pointed out here that a short-fiction award is almost as good as a novel award for these purposes. While you don't have a book you can label an award-winning novel, you certainly can label *yourself* an award-winning writer on everything that comes out, and by the time the copywriters are through, the effect, if any, will be much the same.

Short stories you can campaign for, by the simple expedient of placing them where they reach the highest proportion of nominators and voters. On the track record, this is *Analog*, *F&SF*, and the late-lamented *Orbit*. So many short stories are published in so many places and the nominations are so diffuse that prominence of publication matters at least as much as relative literary merit, and there's not much anyone can do about this. The path to quick awards is through the production of many short stories and their publication in the right places; you *can* make your reputation without writing novels. Whether you can keep from starving to death while doing it is another question.

As for campaigning for an sf novel, the only way I can see to really do this is to try and make sure a large number of the right readers get to read it as soon as possible. For the Nebula in particular, it's an advantage to be published early in the year, and the max exposure never hurt any candidates for the others. If your novel appears first in hardcover, it would be nice to have the paperback out in time for the Hugo voting. On a hardcover, the publisher should get out as many advance galleys as possible, ditto but less importantly for a paperback, and in the case of paperbacks, an SFWA freebie mailing is desirable. A large number of on-sale copies doesn't hurt either.

So if awards are important to you, choose a publisher who gets out a lot of copies, and is generous with freebies, and will publish your book early in the calendar year. Other than that, I don't see how anyone can really affect the outcome by any kind of campaigning. I don't believe that getting loaded at every con held in the universe will really make a difference. You can't afford to buy votes, and what do you really get by asking your friends to vote for you? If they want to, they will; if they don't, they won't, whether you ask them to or not.

So actually, there really isn't anything immoral to do that can be effective. Leaving us with the question of just how important awards are and how one should regard them for sanity's sake.

It depends upon what value you place on them. If it's all a matter of cynical economic advantage, then they help, but maybe not decisively. A book that has 200,000 copies in print is more likely to win an award than an award is likely to generate a distribution of 200,000 copies. A major award is good for an increase in your next advance, but a socko sales record is obviously better.

Finally, then, what are these awards worth in an ultimate sense? How deeply is it sane to have your ego involved in the winning and losing of same? What do they really measure? Except for the Hugo and the Nebula, they represent the considered opinion of comparatively a handful of people. How much you internalize the judgment of the various juries should depend upon the credibility of the jury in your eyes before you know the results. The Hugo is a measure of a work's popularity among attendees and supporting members of the Worldcon, and your judgment of this award should be based upon your opinion of the sagacity of this demographic universe. The Nebula should come as close to being an absolute standard as is theoretically possible to get, being awarded entirely by fellow practitioners of the art, but theory and practice do not necessarily always coincide, especially when the rules are subject to so much mutation.

As for me, I admit that I will happily accept any award that comes my way, but reserve my own final judgment in secret. Since I can't see any way of effectively campaigning, I have no moral problem in that area, and I can yearn and lust and drool with a clean conscience. If you keep a reasonable perspective on what these things really are, there's no real harm in wanting to win, and taking pleasure in it if you do.

Only one thing bothers me. In 1980 there looks to be the best crop of sf novels in many a moon. Those of us who have works in contention may end up secretly wishing it weren't so, that the competition wasn't so strong. Each potential award candidate will no doubt, at least at one point, find themselves wishing that *all those other good novels* hadn't appeared.

Do you think that maybe there's something wrong with that situation?

JUNE 1980
COLUMN 8

How, you may ask, does it feel to learn that you've helped whip ABC and Paramount one day, be elected President of SFWA the next, and only five days later lose to a chicken? On Thursday, I fly from New York to Los Angeles for the Nebula banquet, sleep over that night at Harlan Ellison's; and on Friday morning am there when Henry Holmes, Harlan's lawyer, calls to tell him that they've won a $337,000 judgment against Paramount, ABC, and Terry Keegan in the *Brillo* plagiarism case. Saturday, the Nebula event at the Beverly Wilshire, where I become President-elect of SFWA. The next Thursday, back in New York, the American Book Awards ceremonies, where Fred Pohl's *JEM* wins the hardcover sf award and *The Tale of the Dun Cow*—a religious allegory featuring talking barnyard animals and starring a rooster—wins the paperback sf award, beating out, among other things, my collection, *The Star Spangled Future.*

What the fuck does it all *mean?*

Is this the big time?

Well, what Harlan, Ben Bova, Henry Holmes and associates did to the powers that be in Hollywood with more than a little help from their friends sure as shit is. I'll let someone else go into the legal issues of the *Brillo* case, but the point here is the moment, when for me, the David and Goliath perspective reversed itself. I mean, here are a couple of lowly sf writers suing a major network and a major studio, little guys going up against the unconquerable Establishment, right?

Well, right and wrong. On the day I'm to testify, I'm walking up the courthouse steps with Harlan and Frank Herbert, who is also going to testify that day. Isaac Asimov's deposition has already been read. Ray Bradbury, rebuttal witness, is starting to loosen up in the bullpen.

And the thought comes to me: it's Paramount, ABC, and Keegan who are out of their depth and sure to get creamed. Henry Holmes has trotted out David Gerrold, Ben Bova, Frank Herbert, Harlan Ellison, Isaac Asimov, and Norman Spinrad, and he's going to wind up with Ray Bradbury and all poor John Davies, the defense attorney, has been able to come up with in the way of expert witnesses is a few anonymous professors who are doing it for the money.

Later, it turns out that Davies, a good and honorable man defending clients who are neither, had the same feeling too. These science fiction guys are like some kind of mafia, he confides to Henry at one point, intimating that somehow it isn't fair to poor defenseless Paramount and ABC. Steal from one of them and a whole parade of heavies lines up ready to march into court in jackboots. And no one of stature will testify for the other side, even for *money.*

Now although Harlan is loudly a non-member of SFWA and

has just as loudly proclaimed that he is NOT a science fiction writer, that is NOT how the media coverage is calling it. SCI FI WRITERS WIN PLAGIARISM SUIT AGAINST ABC AND PARAMOUNT shriek the headlines, and in the body of the stories, the names of the expert witnesses are prominently featured along with their sf identification.

So as incoming President of SFWA I feel no compunction in using this karma where it may seem useful. Like in dealing with snots in grievance situations who come on like "Oh, you science fiction writers, you're the guys who publish in all those funny little magazines and sleazy paperback books, huh kid?"

Wrong, asshole, we're the guys who pounded Paramount and ABC into the ground, and incidentally the SFWA is the only writers' organization ever to audit a publisher, out of whom we extracted a quarter mil in back royalties, sucker!

The Nebula banquet and the American Book Awards all in one week is something else again. TABA replaced the National Book Award this year, and loud was the controversy in the New York Literary Establishment and the publishing industry. In fact, what the controversy was *really* all about was the passing of control of the major national book award from the self-appointed New York Literary Establishment to the publishing industry as a whole and the resulting changes.

The old National Book Award was given in only two or three categories by a panel of three—count 'em three—judges. In 1973, when Leslie Fiedler was one of the judges, one of the books he wanted considered for the novel award was *The Iron Dream,* but the other two judges refused to even read it because it was science fiction. I'm not making this up. Fiedler told this story on the William F. Buckley show, and it neatly sums up the attitude of the old NBA to science fiction, so we should all be among those gladly spitting on the corpse of the National Book Award.

The American Book Awards are given in about three dozen categories, science fiction among them. There were separate nominating juries in each category composed of writers, critics, editors, booksellers and librarians knowledgeable in each field, and a final ballot listing all the nominees in all the categories was distributed to 2500 of the volunteers from all regions of the writing and publishing universe who agreed to have their names put in the hat.

So far, a vast improvement over the old NBA.

But not exactly perfect. For one thing, all 2500 voters were enfranchised to vote for the winners in *all* categories, though they were asked not to vote in categories where they were ignorant. The vast silence in the large audience that greeted the announcement of each sf nominee indicated that most of the 2500 potential voters knew nothing about the science fiction nominees, and how many ignoramuses voted is open to conjecture.

For another thing, there were awards for both paperback and hardcover sf books, ostensibly to honor the equality of paperback publishing. However, paperback reprints of last year's hardcovers are co-eligible with paperback originals, and this seems to me like pure economic politics. In fact, last year's failure of *The World According to Garp* to win the NBA was one of the impetuses for creating the American Book Awards, and sure enough it won in the paperback general fiction category.

And in the paperback sf category, another reprint of a hardcover, *The Tale of the Dun Cow,* won the award. Curiously enough, these were probably both the most heavily hyped and massively reprinted paperbacks in their respective categories.

It seems to me that two rule changes are in order. One, the paperback categories should be restricted to paperback *originals* in the future; it certainly does not honor the equality of paperback publishing to grant hardcover books two years of eligibility to only one for paperback originals. Two, there should be separate ballots for the final vote in each category distributed to a voting universe with some sort of knowledge in each. Otherwise, in categories like science fiction, mysteries, etc., you will have a lot of people voting for the only book they heard of—that is, on the basis of hype—or for the candidate of the publishing house they happen to work for. Further, if there are fewer people voting for each category, the publishers can feasibly distribute copies of all the nominees in the category to the voters, so that there is a stronger chance of a more informed vote.

Now as to my short-story collection losing to a chicken....
First of all, I was amazed that *The Star Spangled Future* was a nominee at all. I was even more amazed that of the five nominees in the paperback sf category, two, my book and John Varley's *The Persistence of Vision,* were unequivocally collections of short stories, and a third, Samuel R. Delaney's *Tales of Neveryon,* was either a short-story collection or a novel cleverly disguised as a short-story collection.

It seems that the literary world at large was recognizing something that many of us have long known—namely that science fiction publishing is the last viable refuge of the long and honorable tradition of the American short story. This might give the genre some food for thought when it comes to the categories for our own in-group book awards. It also might give some pause to the people who give out the O. Henry Awards for short fiction of all sorts. The fact is that this award ignores sf, where, I would submit, not merely some but most of the best American short fiction is to be found these days.

The other weird thing about the paperback sf American Book Award is that, in my opinion, there was only *one* unequivocal science fiction novel among the nominees, namely *Dreamsnake*. The winner, *The Tale of the Dun Cow,* is not science fiction, or even sf in form, content, style, or spirit. What makes an allegorical religious animal fable science fiction? Answer: It was bought by Pocket Books sf editor, David Hartwell, and under the rules, the publisher is the one who chooses what category to submit books in.

Why did David chose to submit *The Dun Cow* as a science fiction book? Why did eleven judges accept it as same?

It seems to me that this points sharply to a trend that has been sneaking up on us for about a decade. Used to be that fantasy novels were hardly publishable at all, at least in paperback. Publishers did not perceive an audience for them. Then came the vastly successful publication of the Tolkien books, first by Ace and Don Wolheim, and then by the Ballantines, houses and editors heavily identified with science fiction. They were marketed under a kind of shoehorned expansion of the sf genre category and burst through the top of the sf sales pattern. Then came Lin Carter's line of Fantasy Classics for Ballantine, into which snuck some modern original fantasy novels. Segueing into Conan and the sword and sorcery genre explosion, and now, all this stuff has by accident of history become part of the expanded sf genre, bought and edited by science fiction editors, counted on the sf lists of the various houses, advertised in the sf media, and generally accepted as sf by the "sf community."

That *The Tale of the Dun Cow* won the American Book Award for "best paperback sf book" is only the logically extreme extension of this phenomenon. Now, it would seem, any novel set in something other than the "real" present or the "real" past, that is to say any "non-mainstream" novel is by publishers' category definitions science fiction or at least sf.

Further, it was generally agreed at the editors' panel at the Nebula affair that "fantasy" outsells "science fiction" in the "sf genre," all things being equal, by a factor of about 10%. The tail is already starting to wag the dog.

What this phenomenon will end up doing to science fiction in a literary and philosophical sense is something else again. Philosophically, esthetically, and content-wise, something like *The Tale of the Dun Cow* is further from any non-commercial definition of "science fiction" than most "mainstream" work. It has nothing to do with science, technology, the future, or any of the other generally recognized parameters of science fiction. Yet, according to TABA, it is the best paperback science fiction book of the year.

I'm not sure whether this is good or bad. In an ideal world, there would be no genre categories, and things like *The Dun Cow, Dreamsnake, On Wings of Song* and *The World According to Garp* would be judged against each other for something like the American Book Award as novels, period, strictly on relative quality.

But in the real world, it may force us to open the horrid question of "what *is* science fiction" when it comes to deciding eligibility for things like the Hugos and Nebulas.

I once defined science fiction as "anything published as science fiction." But I must admit that that's beginning to make less and less sense.

However, I must also admit that a new definition, a new operative definition, is a can of worms that I for one am afraid to open.

And that's what it feels like to lose to a chicken.

SEPTEMBER 1980
COLUMN 10

This is being written the week after the Noreascon, the World Science Fiction Convention in Boston, attended by over a hundred of sf's great, near-great, and decidedly un-great literary figures, most of the sf editorial infrastructure, a handful of foreign sf editors, the sf trade press, major and minor fanzine editors, a few reporters from other media (even from Japan), artists, agents, hucksters, and upwards of 7000 fans. Book deals were made and unmade. Foreign rights connections were made. SFWA conducted its major annual meeting under the aegis of yours truly. Books were hyped. Writers were hyped. The Hugos were awarded. Writers hyped their own books. Writers hyped themselves. All in an atmosphere of continuous partying, lubricated by oceans of booze and fogbanks of dope. Assignations were made and broken. Relationships began and ended. There was surprisingly little violence or vomiting, though of course there was some of both.

All this in addition to the programming, which included the Hugo ceremonies, the guest-of-honor speeches, and endless overlapping panels, ranging, in the case of my participation alone, from "Why I Hate Fandom" to "Homophobia in Science Fiction," from stand-up comedy to a level of seriousness that was truly impressive on the subject the discussion of which at such an event would have been inconceivable three years ago.

All in the space of roughly four days and four nights.

By now, of course, science fiction writers and editors and artists take this sort of thing for granted. It's a Worldcon, that's what it is, and so what?

Well, in terms of the purview of this column, survival as a science fiction writer, so quite a lot. No other writers in the history of this planet have experienced anything even remotely like this. We science fiction writers tend to forget that most of our literary colleagues outside the genre lead relatively solitary lives surrounded by public anonymity. Many writers don't even know very many other writers. There may be a dozen writers in the United States with public name recognition value, and maybe three or four with face recognition value from talk show appearances. Before the general public, most writers are as anonymous as we are, except for a few superstars like Vidal, Mailer, and Capote. And even Vidal, Mailer and Capote have never had the experience of being surrounded by 7000 people *all* of whom know your name, the majority of whom know your face, thousands of whom are seeking your autograph, and hundreds of whom seem to know you on a first-name basis. Rock stars may experience this for an evening, but only science fiction writers live such a reality for close to a week at a time.

That's the good news for science fiction writers. By Harry, no other writers in the world get to egotrip like we do! Leave us not forget that fandom invented the very concept of egoboo, and what's available to us is what's available to most writers as sherry is to cocaine.

Moreover, it must be admitted that meaningful contact with one's readers on a human level is also possible to a degree unique to the sf pocket universe. What other writers get to trade more or less affectionate family insults with several hundred of their readers on a "Why I Hate Fandom" panel? What other writers even have a fandom to hate? I have had few experiences more meaningful than being the only straight on a panel on homophobia in a roomful of people confronting their sexual differences from within the greater solidarity of sf and feeling no tension either on the panel or in the audience, at least not on any interpersonal level. Where else is that likely to happen?

The bad news for science fiction writers may be that large science fiction conventions, and the Worldcon in particular, are a lot more central to our careers than is good for our mental health or artistic clarity.

We party with most of the editors and critics in the field. When we do panels, we are *performing* in front of not only our fans, but our colleagues and the people who buy and evaluate our work. The Hugos are awarded in this atmosphere. Deals are made. Perceptions of writers are created, not only in the eyes of the fans, but in the eyes of "the industry." Significant portions of sf publishers' advertising and promotion budgets (such as they are) are spent in the market circumscribed by cons and fanzines.

So let's take a peek at the economic and publishing aspects of what goes on at a Worldcon.

For one thing, with the increasing size of cons and the decreasing purchasing budgets of libraries, the Worldcon can now have a significant impact on the sales of a hardcover sf novel. Is it really unreasonable to assume that 10% to 20% of the attendees might be persuaded to buy a book if it wins the Hugo or if its author makes a big splash in some other way at a Worldcon? We're talking about 700 to 1000 additional sales in a field where 5000 sales is not an unsuccessful hardcover. This is not necessarily a bad thing, of course, but it does mean that panel appearances are in the process of becoming plums of pecuniary importance and that an ad budget designed to secure a Hugo can justify itself in hardcover sales. Not to mention the fact that an award on the cover will not only sell more paperbacks but will greatly enhance the paperback rights price should those rights have been sequestered until the Worldcon.

Furthermore, there seems to be a leveraging effect on paperback sales, even if the paperback has been published before the Hugos. A Hugo should be good for a new printing of at least 25,000 copies. If this puts the distribution of the book up past a critical point of say about 150,000 copies, it will probably mean that the book can stay in print permanently at 20,000 or so sales a year.

As the Worldcons and cons in general increase in size, sf seems to be developing an "alternate economy" of its own. Already, hardcover novels can be made or broken within this sphere. Already, paperbacks can be leveraged into remaining permanently in print. And already, there is a large speculative market in "sf art," a whole new alternate universe of collectors actually investing in the stuff for profit.

It becomes difficult for writers and editors alike to remember that fandom isn't the world.

It isn't, you know.

If there are 10,000 con-going, fanzine-reading fans in the U.S. that represents the upper limit. If each and every one of them bought a copy of a given paperback book or an issue of a given sf magazine, *and nobody else did,* it would be a monumental commercial disaster.

A saturation fanzine and convention advertising and promotion campaign isn't going to sell much more than 15,000 additional copies of anything, allowing for word-of-mouth expansion. Unless, of course, a Hugo is secured to embellish the cover, which can happen to only one book a year.

But when editors and writers meet in a supercharged, boozed-up, stoned-out pocket universe of 7000 fans for a looong weekend, perspective can be lost by editors and writers alike. The 50,000 purchasers of some successful sf novel are anonymous abstracts; the 7000 fans are surrounding you.

It becomes rather easy for editors, observing the performances of writers on panels, the length of the lines at the autograph tables, and the traffic in the huckster room, to tend to judge the marketability of a writer's work by his popularity—forgetting that what is being observed is popularity among a demographically minor segment of the total potential readership. It also becomes easy for an editor to take approval of his line or magazine from the fans—perhaps with a Hugo—as approval from the readership at large.

What this can lead to is a skewing of advances in favor of convention stars and fanzine lions. What it long has definitely led to is the packaging of sf books and magazines to appeal to the tastes of the fannish subculture, the perception of which is read from con art shows and the general vibes in the air.

In some cases, what this has led to, and will continue to lead to, is some expensive flops. Some books that appeal mainly to the hardcore sf readership have been bought for big bucks. Some of these have been packaged for the genre, promoted at cons and advertised in the sf press. These have for the most part done well. By the standards of the field. But not well enough to justify six-figure advances. Some of them have been packaged with "mainstream" covers to try to break through the top of the genre chart, and most of them have flopped by those standards.

All too easy, then, by this perspective, to conclude that six-figure advances can't be justified, and that the best thing to do is continue to use hardcore sf packaging for everything.

So when a real breakout sf novel comes along, one with literary appeal beyond the hardcore sf readership and therefore with sales potential beyond top sf expectations, the tendency may be to restrict it to fannish tastes, or publishers' perceptions of same.

And of course, for writers, perspective can become even more distorted by the fleshly immediacy of the Worldcon. Regardless of other factors, writers want the paperbacks of their hardcovers to be published in time to affect the Hugo voting. Newer writers may gain instant fannish success and lose all perspective on the true literary or even commercial merit of their work. Any number of truly bad writers have their adulatory fannish coteries. Any number of writers who aren't selling zilch may become convinced that they are the "Bradbury of the 1980s" or the second coming of Robert Heinlein if a hundred people tell them so in the space of a weekend. Writers are encouraged to repeat the same good old familiar settings and characters known and loved by the adulatory throng.

So how to make sense of all this and keep your head from being bent out of useful shape? Well, perhaps the best thing is to try to experience the Worldcon as a separate reality, a thing completely unto itself, and not a microcosm of the sf readership at large. In truth, it is one of the compensatory joys of being a science fiction writer to be gifted with a patent of nobility in this little Mittleuropean Grand Duchy where you and all your colleagues are lords of the manor and the citizenry sings informed hosannas.

But beyond the cozy walls of the castle, the world is great and wide, and it, not the Worldcon, is where the higher challenges lie, is where the fate of your fortune lies, is the true arena of your literary adventure.

And above all, feel a chill in your heart the next time some fan walks past you wearing one of those T-shirts which proclaims that "Reality is a crutch for those who can't handle science fiction."

PART FOUR
CRITICISM AND MEDIA ACCESS

This may seem like a large topic for such a small section: only two columns, one on literary criticism within the sf genre apparatus, and one on the New York Literary Establishment as exemplified by the New York Times Book Review. But many issues relating to it will surface again in the section on ART AND COMMERCE and in HOW THINGS WORK.

It is interesting to note that I wrote the piece on the failures of the "Establishment" media to cover sf first, and only later perceived certain congruent problems within the sf critical apparatus itself. Maybe that's because I myself was reviewing science fiction for Destinies when I wrote the piece on the NYLE and couldn't look critically at my own sphere of critical discourse until I had at least temporarily left it. Of course the failure of the Establishment media vis-a-vis sf is much older and more complete than the breakdown in the genre critical apparatus. Nevertheless, I've arranged these columns in what happens to be reverse chronological order because it seems to make more sense to deal with the microcosm before going on to the macrocosm.

The 1981 Hugo nominees referred to in the first column of this section and in the first section of ART AND COMMERCE are:

The Snow Queen by Joan Vinge (The Hugo winner)
Lord Valentine's Castle by Robert Silverberg
Ringworld Engineers by Larry Niven
Beyond the Blue Event Horizon by Frederick Pohl
Wizard by John Varley

DECEMBER 1981
COLUMN 16

Perusing the complex Hugo voting results tables in *Locus* #249, I was struck by a strange intuition. I checked it out. It was true. I flipped to the *Locus* best-seller list. Son of a bitch, same thing there!

Good reviews have no correlation with either the Hugo results or the best-seller list anymore. Except maybe a negative one.

Now understand that in other incarnations, I have been both the recipient of reviews as a novelist over the last couple of years, and a reviewer myself, in *Destinies,* so I have been looking at all the significant regular sf reviewing, such as it is, and have a pretty good perception of the general flow. So while the following is not based on a computerized statistical study, I think one would verify this general picture within a 10% margin of error.

Of the five Hugo nominees for novel, not one could have been said to have received unanimous or even general rave reviews, three of them received generally mixed reviews, and two of them could be said to have received more negative critical attention than positive acclaim. One must go down to seventh place in the nominations list before finding a novel published to a chorus of hosannas.

As far as the August *Locus* best-seller list, the situation is even more weirdly extreme, or extremely weird, or more precisely, both. Of the top ten paperbacks, only one was a critical rave, a second was a Stephen King book which inhabits another critical reality, three got mixed reviews, and the rest hardly got any critical attention at all. The hardcover list is a somewhat less extreme example of the same situation.

You can read it in the bottom line. Reviews, at least in this current slice of time, seem to have little or no effect on either the acclaim of the regular convention-going fans as expressed in the Hugos, or the extended science fiction readership as expressed in sales.

I don't know about you, but I find this extremely weird. There certainly was a time when this wasn't so. Granted that a certain amount of bad work inevitably wins any popularity contest, and granted in spades that a great deal of crap moves briskly on the racks, still there was a time when general critical praise was instrumental in the awards and at the very least a general Bronx cheer was counterproductive to same.

Now of course, you are saying, wait a minute, who says that

the critics don't promulgate a certain amount of their own bad work too? All too true. This is not a discussion of the effect of criticism as an unerring measure of intrinsic literary worth, but of reviews as promotion, of the impact, or lack of it, of what we have thought of as the main media through which sf readers gain their consumer information about what is offered for their purchase. As well as how these media do or do not move the consensus towards awards.

What media? The national publications which regularly review science fiction, of course. Such as they are. Namely *Analog, Fantasy & Science Fiction, Asimov's, Twilight Zone,* and *Amazing.* Short list, isn't it? The total circulation figures aren't exactly overwhelming either, far short of half a million, and that with a high degree of overlap. In addition, we have *Locus* and *Starship* with minimal circulation in these terms, but with a highly-motivated readership of pros and fannish tastemakers, intermittent occasional pieces in *Omni,* and quickies in *Heavy Metal. Future Life,* I have just been told, is defunct.

Science fiction, as we all surely know, receives very little attention either in the news magazines or the media apparatus of the New York Literary Establishment, save for the occasional *sui generis* exception. For all practical purposes, these five sf magazines, a handful of other publications, and the fanzines, *are* the critical environment into which most science fiction novels are launched.

Since the biggest circulation among the regulars is in the 100,000 range, which is to say in the range of what one top or near-top-selling sf novel must net, one can see that it's a bit difficult for the tail to wag the dog. In other words, a commercially successful sf novel sells more copies than a commercially viable sf magazine, so obviously there are a lot of book buyers who don't read the magazines at all. So it's not so hard to see why reviews are pretty irrelevant to the *Locus* best-seller list.

But it's not so easy to see why they seem to be becoming irrelevant to the Hugo too. After all, anyone who's sufficiently obsessed with science fiction to go to the Worldcon and vote for the Hugos surely must be more than an occasional reader of more than one of the sf magazines. Why then do we read a lack of effect of the criticism therein on this award?

The medium may be the message, but in this case the medium is hitting the readership, but the message isn't coming through. Or to put it another way, the critics do not seem to share the taste of the readership. There is no dialectic between them.

What is the nature of current sf criticism anyhow? *Fantasy &
Science Fiction* provides continuity with a tradition that included
Anthony Boucher, Damon Knight, Alfred Bester, and Avram
Davidson in the form of Algis Budrys, with occasional fine relief
pitching from such as Barry Malzberg and Joanna Russ. Here we
have analysis of a kind and a certain grasp of the literary history
of the field.

A combination which seems to exist nowhere else. Theodore
Sturgeon provides capsule consumer reports for *Twilight Zone.*
Analog's review column has lately been shared by two fiction
writers at early stages of their careers, and *Amazing* has a
reviewer of similar description. *Asimov's* reviewer tends toward
roundup reviews of literarily insignificant books, and is not
much concerned with any critical generality.

With the exception of the *F&SF* crew, there is no regular
critic working in the field on the professional level of the best of
the writers whose books he is judging, or even of the general run
of books worthy of critical consideration. Which is not to say
these people are incapable of perceptive reviews from time to
time, only that none of them has the stature of the work they are
criticizing.

Broadly speaking, there are two kinds of criticism: consumer
reports aimed at readers, and critical analysis aimed at least
partly at writers, and therefore at the improvement of the breed.
Of the latter, there is a tremendous dearth in the sf genre
currently. As witness the birth of such journals as *Venom,* in
which writers of stature go at each other and sometimes
themselves under the cloak of pseudonyms, and *Patchin Review,*
in which some serious and thoughtful stuff exists cheek by jowl
with an invidious gossip column and challenges to literary duels.
Surely the existence of such all-pro fanzines and their rather
shrill natures indicates that the writers of science fiction lack a
sense of confidence in the credibility of the current critics.

It wasn't always so. When Algis Budrys and Damon Knight
and Schulyer Miller and Judy Merril and John Clute and M. John
Harrison and Michael Moorcock and Avram Davidson and so
forth were more or less actively reviewing in the same geological
era, one waited with a certain more heightened expectation for
the verdict of one's peers. Indeed, it was more than a matter of
verdict or the angle of attack, there was always the possibility
that one might learn something useful in the evolution of one's
craft.

Now, alas, Budrys and his relievers at *F&SF,* from the point of view of working writers, stick out like sore thumbs as the atavistic remnant of this critical tradition.

Most of the rest of sf reviewing is a critical encounter of the first kind, consumer reporting aimed at the readers. Now one would think that if the magazine reviewers were out of sync with their readership, with the hardcore people who buy magazines, changes would eventually be made. Contrariwise, if what we have here is demographically representative reviewing, then there should be a high correlation between reviews and Hugos.

Weirdly enough, we seem to have neither.

What we seem to have here are several overlapping phenomena. The best-seller list verifies once more what everyone already knows, namely that books have long since become the main medium of sf and the magazines have long since lost their centrality. The Hugo nominations and voting seem to suggest that this has become true even among hardcore con-going fans. It may very well be that the reviewers for the various magazines more or less represent the tastes of the various readerships of those magazines, but it would seem that the tastes of the readers of those magazines no longer represent the taste of either the mass audience for sf novels or the hardcore sf fans.

Of course, many would contend that it is the function even of consumer-oriented criticism to uphold standards and thereby elevate the taste of the readership, to elucidate the worthy but somewhat difficult, and thereby perform an act of education.

But in order for this to happen, the readership must accept the proposition that the critical savants possess some quantity of knowledge and wisdom in literary matters in advance of their own. When the critics were either well-regarded fiction writers themselves, editors of repute, or demonstrated experts of long experience, the reader could accept them more readily as trailblazers without having to accept a loss of private face. Now, however, the review column is more of an entry-level position into the profession of science fiction, and the readership therefore may see itself as equally sage, or to put it another way, may see the reviewer as just a bloke like themselves.

Finally, we have the phenomenon of advertising and convention appearances superseding reviews as the demographic mainline of sf book promotion. After all, reviews are PR too, in the sense that they are one means by which the public is informed of the existence of a book and given an impression of what may be inside the covers before they buy it. Before the advent of advertising budgets for sf, reviews would probably be the only place the name of a book would appear in print in a magazine. Now a publisher can inject at least an awareness and recognition value into the consumer consciousness for any book he chooses by taking ads in the same publications that print reviews, or even in publications that don't and which reach larger audiences. Similarly, convention appearances can become the low-budget equivalent of the talk show circuit, impressing the public personality of the writer-performer upon the product itself.

In other words, certain of the lower critical functions have been taken over by marketing, and certain of the higher critical functions have been largely surrendered to the void.

Thus the state of the critical apparatus of the sf genre, alienated both from the working writers and from the readership for their books. Thus do we find dark hothouse mutants like *Venom* and *Patchin Review* blooming in the hydroponic tanks of the intellectual life-support system of our sealed little spacecraft. Thus do we find a few of our number bemused and bedazzled by the arcane gibberings to be found in some of the academic sf journals.

Perhaps what we are seeing is one of the results of in-breeding. Over time, isolated communities seem to suffer a certain malaise of the gene pool, a lack of hybrid vigor. As far as the larger critical arena goes, sf might just as well not exist. Therefore, as far as sf goes, the larger critical arena might just as well not exist. As witness such phenomena as the ecstatic hailing of Russell Hoban's *Riddley Walker* as a work of genius by the "mainstream" critical mavens without any awareness of its numerous models within the genre, or Theodore Solatoroff's ignorant praise of Stanislaw Lem as "one of the deep spirits of the age" when he was really extolling the general virtues of science fiction if only he had the wit or knowledge to know it.

Yes, before we start beating our own breasts and howling mea culpas, we should realize that the sorry current state of genre sf criticism owes no little blame to the isolation of the genre from the critical mainstream. What little criticism of science fiction finds its way into the mainstream media makes higher fanzine reviewing look pretty good. And if you think the general run of magazine book reviewing is a matter of inconsequential analysis of the unimportant, take a look at a few weeks' run of *The New York Times Book Review*. If you think this crisis in critical consciousness is a phenomena of the isolated sf genre alone, take a look outside, and think again.

JULY 1980
COLUMN 9

Why does science fiction have such a shitty public image among the literati? And what can be done about it? And how important is it? And who are these people anyway and who elected them the arbiters of what is and is not "serious literature"?

Yes, friends, I'm talking about the fabled New York Literary Establishment, which does in its way exist, and which is and is not important to the destiny of that which we call "science fiction."

In the most narrow technical sense, the NYLE consists of those major national and New York publications which review books at all, the people who edit and write them, certain writers who go to their cons, a few book editors and houses such as Farrar Straus and Knopf who are considered "serious" and "non-commercial" by same, and the assorted Big Name Fans and Supergroupies you would expect.

Consider the power these people have. Book publishing is even more a New York industry than TV is Hollywood, I mean it's *all* in the Big Apple—the publishers, the agents, the national magazines in large part, *Publishers Weekly,* the American Book Awards, The Business. How many national publications review books in the first place? Not that many—*Time, Newsweek, Playboy,* and right away you're starting to drop down into low-circulation "prestige" journals and the science fiction magazines. Book reviews are simply not a major item of mass general-interest journalism.

So a few publications that all have "New York" in their name —*The New Yorker, The New York Review of Books,* the daily *New York Times Book Review Column,* and the leader of the pack, the *New York Times Book Review* itself—have assumed an importance in the world of literature and book publishing all out of proportion to their demographics.

The circulation figures for these magazines combined probably aren't much higher than say *Playboy's* or all the sf-related magazines, yet a review in any one of them is far more important to how a novel does and how it is received than anything but a review in *Time* or *Newsweek.*

Why? How? Que pasa?

Well, for one thing, the *New York Times Book Review* comes out every week and it does nothing but review books. With 52 issues a year at maybe 40 pages per on the average and six daily *NY Times* columns a week to back it up, it may be the only publication extant with the exception of *Publishers Weekly* that can even pretend to cover the ongoing world of books definitively. Which of course it does. In addition to reviews, each issue contains a gossip and business news column on both paperback and hardcover publishing, a letter column, various features, and the potent *New York Times* Best Seller List, an excellent textbook example of the self-fulfilling prophecy.

The Times Best Seller List, of course, lists the top 15 hardcover best sellers in fiction and non-fiction and the top 15 in mass market and trade paperback. For this alone, it attracts the attention of publishers, writers, editors, and advertising departments. At the bottom of the best seller list is a list of runners-up and candidates for same, and also an "Editor's Choice" list of books the *Times* mavens deem worthy, reprinted from a large facing feature of the same name.

Because of all this, the *Times Book Review* commands enormous ad rates in proportion to its demographics, and because of this a review in the *New York Times Book Review* can be the max important to a book, particularly a hardcover. The *Times Book Review* is the *Locus, Variety, Women's Wear Daily,* and *Rolling Stone* of the publishing industry, read by all the movers, shapers, and purchasers of books. A publisher who sees his book get good notice in the *Times Book Review* will be motivated to pump ad money into same. Get "discovered" here and the other NYLE zines will soon follow suit. Librarians read it. Booksellers read it. And "serious general readers" turn to it for what appears to be comprehensive coverage of the weekly world of books.

The *Times Book Review* sits at the top of the literary media pyramid. It is recognized as the major arbiter of "absolute literary merit"-as well as of the literature-commerce interface. To receive serious notice there is to eventually be reviewed in the lesser Establishment zines and local book columns in newspapers all over the country. It is *de rigueur* for major general literary awards.

Thus the "New York Literary Establishment," a community not unlike the sf community, consists of its media, their readership, those intimately interested in what the subculture agrees is "serious literature," and its connections with the industry itself. And, of course, the writers who write the reviews and the books that these people esteem.

Just as a reputation as a "Big Name Pro" is made in the sf community, not on the racks, a reputation as a "major American writer" is made in the New York Literary Community, a community of people who sincerely believe that their collective tastes constitute "absolute literary values" and have the focused media power to sell this notion to the macroculture.

Where does science fiction stand in relation to all this?

We all know where. Way at the back of the bus.

But *why*? Sf is about 15% of the fiction published in the United States, and literarily speaking it encompasses all fiction not set in the present or historical past, which is to say most literature that had better be of central concern to any civilization that hopes to survive into the 21st Century. How can a literary phenomenon of this order be treated as non-existent by American literary mavens?

Well, of course, sf is also a lot of exploitation films, comic books, schlocko covers, fan conventions, and assorted weirdnesses, and when it has been covered by the news media, that is what comes across because that is what is visual and "newsworthy." Sf's own PR has been the media equivalent of hara-kiri. The odious acronym "sci-fi" and the attributes it epitomizes have not helped.

In short, sf has been considered "Pop Literature" by those who distinguish "Pop" from "Serious" since the days of Hugo Gernsback, and as a result an abyss of ignorance has grown within the literary establishment as to what is really written within this mode. And with 500 new titles a year all packaged on the same level, it is difficult for even conscientious and willing outsiders to sort out the wheat from the chaff. Furthermore, the track record shows that that which is greeted with hosannas, big sales figures, and awards within the sf universe is not necessarily written on a level that would survive scrutiny by those who at least profess to defend "absolute literary values."

In grottier terms, it is also true, at least until very recently, that sf has not commanded ad budgets sufficient unto making it a significant economic element in NYLE zines' survival.

So what can be done about it?

Well, now that we have considered the power that the NYLE *does* have, consider what power it *doesn't* have. It does not have demographic power. A good review in *Time* or *Newsweek* can make it redundant. So can a first-class ad campaign. So can five minutes on the Johnny Carson show or Snyder or Cavett. There are more of us than there are of them. Huge conventions and lots of them. A readership in the scientific community. A large media net of fanzines. What is the name of the prototype space shuttle and who dropped enough letters and pressure on a President of the United States to cause it to happen?

If one can reach the stage of detachment where one does not internalize the NYLE's self-appointed role as arbiter of the absolute literary value of one's work, it is not difficult to perceive that what we have here is a question of access to media, of freedom of information, of full and honest reporting, and of economic class interest.

We have a *right*—moral, political, literary, and economic—to demand that science fiction have equal media access with other modes of literary expression. Why the fuck not?

In economic terms, sf is an imporant part of the industry. Why should sf publishers, editors, and writers be second-class citizens of the literary community? Certainly not on the grounds of lack of clout. We may not be regular producers of best sellers, but compare the numbers on an average sf novel with the novel of an average "serious" mainstream novelist, not a superstar. The sf novel figures to do about 5000 in hardcover and come out in a paperback that does maybe 50,000. The literary novel might not even sell 1000 hardcovers, and if it comes out in paper at all, the writer is ahead of the game, which usually must include grants, teaching gigs, and other academic scams. Sf has *readers*. Without ads, or major reviews, or even any reviews at all, science fiction novels can thrive on pure reader interest alone, devoid of hype. We may need Them to break our books out of the ghetto and thus reach our maximum natural audience, but we sure as shit don't need anyone but ourselves to survive, as we've proven for lo these many years in the wilderness.

As to "absolute literary values," I would contend that they simply don't exist, and anyone who claims they are in possession of same are wearing blinders. Certainly anyone who excludes fiction from "serious" consideration on the basis of content alone is either full of shit or exercising a deliberate cultural or political bias. As to questions of style, well, if it doesn't convey meaning to an interested readership of some size, can it really be superior to style that does? One of the great cliches is that sf is short on characterization by the inherent nature of the form. Ridiculous! *All* fiction is about characters if it is going to be fiction at all. "Mainstream" fiction tends to relate characters to their own individual pasts and define them mainly in terms of the evolution of the psyche, whereas sf tends to relate characters to the cultural, scientific, political, and perceptual matrix. Although, of course, either mode can do either or both potentially.

The last resort of the scoundrel, Sturgeon's Law, points out that 90% of sf is shit. But it also points out that 90% of everything is shit, as witness the level of much of the mainstream stuff that *does* get reviewed. But any review policy that pretends to anything like "absolute literary values" must concern itself with the 10%, both of mainstream and of sf.

In the real world, maybe 25 to 50 of the 500 new sf books published each year merit review in places like the *New York Times Book Review,* a couple of dozen books good enough by "absolute" standards to keep company with the likes of Updike, Roth, and various other favored paper tigers.

Finally, what if anything can we do about it? And by we, I mean writers, editors, publishers, devotees, dedicated readers, and merchants of sf. To enumerate us is to make the answer obvious. This situation has existed for a long time; to break out of the ghetto, we must first break out of ghetto thinking.

Previously, we have pissed and moaned about the ghettoization of sf, even while tugging our forelocks in the direction of our oppressors in the forlorn hope of securing sufficient favor to become a "token sf writer." Somewhere deep inside we have accepted the mavens' judgment of sf as minor and "not serious" and of themselves as the gatekeeper of literary Valhalla. By accepting this, we have made it true.

But if we get rid of all that, and see the problem as one of media access pure, dirty, and simple, then the solution becomes obvious. We—the extended we—are not exactly nobody. We are 15% of the publishing industry, and the bread and butter of more than one house. We are 600 writers, and one shudders to think how many active fans. We are any number of scientists of stature, and names like Clarke, Asimov, Heinlein, Bradbury, King, Roddenberry, Ellison, and Co. As well as any number of unknown Big Name Admirers. Collectively, we have economic clout, a certain amount of talk show access, people whose letters cannot simply be confined to the crank file, excellent media of internal communication, and lots of willing footsoldiers for any media war.

If 10% of the energy that a horde of Trekkies put into saving and later resurrecting Star Trek went into forthrightly demanding science fiction's right to access to the literary media, how long could anyone ignore such a manifestation of the public will in a sphere where general public apathy is taken for granted?

PART FIVE
ART AND COMMERCE

This final section on ART AND COMMERCE contains, with one exception, the five most recent STAYIN' ALIVE columns included in this book, arranged in the chronological order in which they were written and published.

When I began writing these columns, I had no idea that I would end up confronting the kinds of issues dealt with in ART AND COMMERCE. I started out dealing with commerce, period. But just as I hope that this book will be a higher educational experience for the reader, so do I know now that the process of writing the columns over time has been an educational experience for me, an outward journey into the pragmatics of publishing, but also an inward journey into the question of the creative facts of life. In the end, "Stayin' Alive" means both economic survival tactics and the art of riding the interface between personal creative impulse and the corporate economic reality without either becoming a pawn in the game or starving to death.

This section begins with a column announcing why I would not be attending the Denver Worldcon, and somehow, the act of performing a public gesture to call attention to a meta-critical position was, in retrospect, a kind of Rubicon for the column.

I felt I had to back analysis with deed because I thought that the very essence of the internal problem of the sf genre that I was addressing was that the sf community was ignoring these areas of extra-economic concern. I felt, in short, that reintroducing such concerns into the discourse would be a hard sell.

I was to be pleasantly surprised. I received support from

many writers—beginning writers who showed a high degree of literary idealism and even some old pros who carefully told me that they agreed with most of what I was saying even though they calculated it impolitic to say so in public. Though quite a few did say so in public.

After that, the column became much more of a feedback relationship with its audience of science fiction writers and would-be science fiction writers. I learned that many editors read it, some approvingly. People suggested areas of concern. So if the column seems to have drifted from the hard pragmatics of HOW TO, it did so under evolutionary pressure, as an expression and perhaps a catalyst of a feeling growing within the sf community at large that it was time we looked up from our checkbooks long enough to raise artistic and cultural considerations back to a level of conscious attention where they belong.

Since a false alarm would mark one as a swine and an asshole, no one wants to be the first to cry "Fire!" in a crowded theater. As a result, people may stand around while the room begins to fill with smoke. But when someone finally does point out that the joint is on fire, everyone else then feels free to acknowledge the dangerous situation.

Which, of course, they were secretly thinking about all along.

SEPTEMBER 1981
COLUMN 14

It has been pointed out to me by the publisher of a rival journal to Locus that I should clearly disclaim any connection between my opinions expressed as a Locus columnist and official positions taken by SFWA, of which I happen to currently find myself President. This has never really seemed necessary to me until now—I have been careful to exclude SFWA, its policies, and its functions from the purview of this column entirely, a disclaimer of deed rather than purpose.

Now, however, with this piece and columns twelve and thirteen, I find myself approaching the center of what it means to be a science fiction writer in the 1980s, a place where the writer of science fiction, the Locus observer, and the President of SFWA all interface, and at a time when I, Norman Spinrad, the essence behind all three of these functional avatars, find it necessary for reasons which this column will, I hope, explain, to back words with deed.

Thus I hereby declare that the heinous act that I plan to

commit relects neither official SFWA policy nor the policy of this magazine nor anything else but my own personal imperative.

I will not attend the Denver Worldcon.

Why will I not attend the Denver Worldcon? That such a bizarre act of omission would seem to the readership of this column to require an explanation, that not appearing at the Worldcon would seem to require a disclaimer that this does not represent SFWA policy, is, in a way, sufficient reason in and of itself.

When I was vice president of the SFWA around 1973 or so, I was of the rather forceful opinion that official SFWA business meetings or other functions should not be held at science fiction conventions, that the professional organization representing science fiction professionals should have no formal connection with cons put on by sf fans. Since this was and is clearly a minority opinion, I have made no attempt as President to change the existing policy, and will make no such attempt. There *will* be an SFWA business meeting at Denver; I simply will not chair it. And what follows, therefore, is emphatically *not* an official position of the President of SFWA.

In the 1970s, I was hard put to explain precisely why I believed that an organization of science fiction professionals should have no formal or official connection with sf conventions in general and the Worldcon and its Hugos in particular. All I had was perhaps prescient intuition that this was a very bad idea. Now, as we enter the 1980s, the specifics begin to come into focus.

As detailed previously, three out of the five nominees for Hugo for best sf novel of this year are sequels. I've since learned that the other two nominees, *The Snow Queen* and *Lord Valentine's Castle*, will soon be revealed as prequels to another round of sequels. When all novels nominated for the Hugo turn out to be episodes of series, it is mathematically certain that we are not dealing with chance but with a consistent devolution in the level of aspiration of science fiction writers intimately bound up with the whole apparatus of science fiction publishing, fandom, conventions, and Hugos.

What we are seeing, among other things, is the disappearance, or at the very least the decline, of commercially middling sf novels as the backbone of sf publishing. On the high end, we have the emergence of the occasional sf best seller like *God Emperor of Dune,* the forthcoming Sagan novel, and any sf written by Stephen King. On the low end, we have, essentially, all other sf book publishing, with ad budgets declining from an already low base, downward pressure on advances, separate sf lines isolated from the rest of publishing by special brand names, logos, and sleazoid uniform packaging.

Since, in the publishing macrocosm, the "middle list" novel has already become a vanishing species, this should hardly be surprising. Ideally, publishers would love to publish *nothing* but best sellers.

Each of us as reader comes complete with a pattern of social programming imprinted upon our consciousness by the media of the macrocosm and the milieu of whatever voluntary subcultures we have chosen to inhabit. Each of us also has overlayed upon this generality psychic structures that are the result of our own personal histories. These patterns are, if you will, the emotional buttons, the reflex arcs available to writers desiring to evoke patterns of ersatz emotional responses that are the essence of fictional experience.

There are only two strategies available to writers of fiction. One may use images, plot-skeletons, words, key phrases, fictional events, and patterns designed to push the buttons in time-tested sequences of tension and release not unlike the stylized performance of sexual intercourse and thereby reassuringly produce the expected literary orgasm as the hero or heroine triumphs over adversity in the thrilling conclusion. This is the technique of writing a best seller. Or one may use images, techiques, words, and so forth to reveal to the reader the pattern of his own buttons, and by extension those of the social realm which has formed them. This is the technique of writing true literature, and, until recently, of seriously intended science fiction.

Since the former produces tension-release, reassurance, and the spurious illusion of enlightenment while the latter produces often uncomfortable insights, pushing the buttons, on the whole, will always have in general a greater mass popularity than elucidating the mechanisms.

Sf fans have always professed to prefer the latter, going so far as to dub the resulting effect the evocation of "sense of wonder." Best sellers, by their very nature, tend to have large short-term sales, and then to vanish into the dustbin of history, since most of them are essentially interchangeable rehashings of the same psychic pattern, i.e., the "plot skeleton." Successful literature, including successful science fiction, tends to have smaller short-term sales but also tends to last, speaking as it does to the essential spirit rather than to the programmed overlay.

Which is why the disappearance of commercially middling

novels in publishing at large is a cultural disaster to the society at large, and the decline of commercially middling sf novels is a disaster to those of us who care about the spirit of science ficiton.

The perceptive reader will have noted that I have oversimplified the situation. Actually, of course, the best seller strategies of tension-release plot-skeletons, wish-fulfillment heros, spurious transcendence, and climactic reassuring literary orgasm have long been the formula of *all* commercial fiction, not excluding most sf. The difference between, say, Harold Robbins and Doc Smith, is not a matter of literary intent but of accessibility of imagery and setting, the self-fulfilling prophecy of commercial expectation, and level of technical craftsmanship.

In theory, the apparatus of fans, conventions, and Hugos should serve to separate the essential grain from the fad-blown chaff, and however imperfectly, this has tended to happen in the past. *Dune,* for example, originally dropped dead in hardcover and took many years to build its formidable paperback sales. The existence of a subculture of sf-obsessed fanatics with their own private media allowed many worthy books to survive their immediate lack of conspicuous commercial success in the macrocosm.

Now, however, the Hugo nominations for novel at the Denver Worldcon tell a different and sadder tale, the apotheosis of the invasion of sf by the best seller strategy from top to bottom, to the detriment of the middle, which should be the heart of the genre.

Anyone who has been reading these columns knows that non-best seller sf publishing is in the process of becoming ghettoized through sf line-names, logos, and cereal-box consistent packaging, and you didn't have to read it here to know that series novels have come to dominate the genre. But *why?*

Obviously because sf publishers perceive this strategy as commercially optimum. Publish those sf novels with near-surething best seller potential as best sellers outside the sf line and publish everthing else as sections of interchangeable cultural product. *Why?*

Why not? The same process, and at more advanced stages of evolution, has infected publishing in general, film, and television.

Why?

In the 1960s, popular culture purveyed "mind-blowing" product, which is to say fiction, music, cinema, and to a much lesser degree TV, which *revealed* the underlying cultural mindsets instead of stroking them. In the 1970s, the mind-blown masses metamorphosed into the "Me Generation," seekers after new mind-sets, refugees from the psychic chaos of excessive psychic freedom. The popular media began to portray and legitimize this flight from freedom. The obvious next step was a popular culture purveying reassurance, nostalgia, and a return to ritualization of the dialectic between the individual psyche and the social matrix.

Thus (incredibly enough if you dare confront the reality) sf, supposedly the literature of the future, of change, of ongoing transcendent evolution, has come not merely to be invaded but now dominated by neomedievalism, elitist fantasy, dragons, and an anti-democratic, anti-scientific, indeed anti-rational nostalgia for the non-existent good old days of evil wizards and mighty-thewed warriors of both sexes.

The vogue for series novels so glaringly pinpointed by the Hugo nominations only translates this essentially fascist nostalgia into cynical commercial strategy. How better, commercially speaking, to pander to this nostalgic flight from freedom than to channel its energy into nostalgia for the last episode and sales for the next?

The essence of the best seller strategy of a literature of reassurance is that the mind-set of the reader must be neither challenged nor changed by the reading process, though it is desirable to create the illusion of some sort of transcendence. Neomedievalist pseudo-mystical fantasy does this quite nicely; such stuff done up in pseudo-scientific drag does it even better; and a science-fantasy series which evokes nothing beyond nostalgia for its own alienated frame of reference is well-nigh perfect.

Of course if you are *really* greedy, you can carry the process one step further and reduce the entire genre to a cliched generality utterly insulated from winds of change. Then, perhaps, you can, by packaging your sf line in a manner that insures that brand identification supersedes the individual identity of any book within it, transfer the generalized nostalgia into loyalty to your line of goods itself, so that readers no longer search for books by their favorite writers or even for the next episode in their favorite series but for the latest from DAW, Del Rey, Timescape, et. al.

At which point, you no longer have to advertise individual novels, and you will have proletarianized the writers into acceptance of more or less standard advances for more or less interchangeable jobs of work.

Or, as the Japanese aphorism so aptly puts it, "The nail that stands up too high gets hammered down."

So, not without a certain sadness, I will not be attending the Denver Worldcon. I will miss the parties, and the company of good friends and comrades from around the world of science fiction. What I will not miss is the glorification of the very process which is hammering down the sphere of discourse and the sometimes gallant folk within which I have come to love.

No, this is not my announcement that I am "leaving science fiction." Within 18 months, I will publish yet another science fiction novel, whose sales parameters I can now predict within a margin of 10%. Nor do I at all feel financially defeated. Nor will I discontinue this column as long as a need for it is felt.

Nor, even, is this another gesture of contempt for fandom. The fact is that sf fandom, now as always, has the potential to stand as guardian of the true spirit of the genre, the spirit of ongoing evolution, of dedication to something beyond the cynically commercial, of the true sense of wonder which it professes to hold so dear. That the apparatus of fandom, Worldcons, and Hugos now stands accused of collaboration with those very forces which would crush that spirit only points out the potential of its power for good or evil within our little universe.

Finally, perhaps, this is my poor attempt at a message to the new generation of writers entering the genre now. You are striving to establish yourselves as sf writers at a time when the easy access and lavish advances for early works of the middle 1970s are in the process of evaporating. Nevertheless, by playing the game as it has always been played, by cultivating con-going fandom and fanzine editors, by adopting proper professional attitude, crafting your sf novel series, and not making waves, you can hope, some of you, to make a somewhat precarious living as professional sf writers. You might even win a Hugo.

Thus was it ever, except for a brief period at the end of the 1970s. I hope, though, that a few of you, and, in the best of all possible worlds more than a few, may perceive that since the struggle ahead of you is more likely to be one for economic survival than for riches (if money is your goal, TV writing, for example, is easier and far more lucrative), you might as well try to make your sf careers count for more than a precarious living and a few trophies.

If a few of you end up getting the message, then missing a Worldcon will have been more than worth it.

NOVEMBER 1981
COLUMN 15

Having called into question the effect upon the quality of what is published as sf of the entire genre apparatus of logos, brand names, stylized packaging, fandom, fanzines, etc., up to and including the Hugos, ruthless logic would have me consider in this context whether something such as this column has done more harm than good.

When I was first asked to do this column, Charlie Brown's request grew out of a series of articles later published as a booklet on the SFWA Model Paperback Contract. The idea was to educate writers on the business of science fiction. Since the eternal verities of the basic business of being a science fiction writer could obviously be dealt with in a limited number of installments, STAYIN' ALIVE evolved in the direction of a continuous re-evaluation of continuingly evolving market conditions. Since its debut was during the mutational sf boom, there was plenty of evolving to write about.

But now, with hindsight's wisdom, I wonder if, like most of us, I wasn't missing an essential point: if the existence of a column such as this and the perceived need for it wasn't part of the wool that we were all pulling over our eyes.

While we were mesmerized by spiraling advances and how best to secure them, sinister paradigm shifts and devolutions were going on within the literature of the genre itself; and this column, like most sf criticism, gossip, and bullshitting of the period, did little to center them in our collective consciousness.

Only now, with the boom having at the very least platformed out into a new, stable economic and media configuration quite different from what preceded it, are we beginning to stick our noses out of our ledgers and perceive that while we were all attempting to maximize our careers, things were happening to the spirit of our product.

It is both utterly paradoxical and utterly true to say that fantasy now dominates the sf genre. The truth is written large everywhere—in the *Locus* best seller lists, on publishers' sf order forms, in review columns, in the Hugo and even the Nebula nominations, in the submissions coming in over the transom to book editors, in the sacred bottom line.

We all know this has happened. But who of us, if asked to describe the genre of the 1980s at the opening of the 1970s, would have predicted that it would go virtually unnoticed until it was all but completed?

Well back then, there was an editor named Alan Ravage at Bantam, who was editing sf and who presented to me a rather strange evaluation of the submissions he was getting. He was starting to see a flood of what he called "anti-science fiction," and it had him worried. "If you guys don't watch out," he told me, "this stuff is going to take over your market."

What the hell did he mean by "anti-science fiction"? I wanted to know.

What he told me was that he was seeing a lot of stuff that, while targeted at the sf audience, was esthetically, philosophically, and even spiritually antithetical to that literature which was then currently being published as science fiction. Rather than exploring an ongoing evolutionary future, it either harkened back to a bogus pseudo-medievalist past, or constructed an analog of same in a post-collapse future. Rather than attempting the great synthesis of scientific rationality with emotional and spiritual insight, it viewed science as the wicked antithesis of humanistic values. Anti-science fiction in the same sense that a positron is an anti-electron, or a mirror image of the reality it reflects.

This stuff fits into the mood of the time better than science fiction does, the politically and socially concerned Mr. Ravage told me. This is where the country is headed. You guys are going to be in trouble, and I don't know what you're going to do about it.

Now, in the 1980s, of course, we know exactly what we did about it. Alan Ravage proved a puissant prophet in terms of what was going to be published as sf in our time, but he was dead wrong about who was going to be coining a profit off of it. He severely underestimated the ability of sf writers to adapt to economic evolutionary pressure. Sf writers did not lose their audience to a new breed of anti-sf Philistines with their own anti-fans, anti-fanzines, anti-cons, and anti-Hugos, nor were sf lines squeezed out of the racks by anti-sf lines. Rather did the entire sf apparatus spread its legs and adapt to the inevitable with hardly a conscious thought about the process and prospered nicely in the bargain too, thank you.

It is a curious coincidence as well that the rise of fantasy in "sf clothing" has so neatly coincided with the trend towards series novels. Or is it?

If we look at both fantasy and series novels within the sf genre in Alan Ravage's psychosocial terms, as cultural artifacts in a feedback relationship with the mass consciousness they arise out of and service, we see that there are more than coincidental similarities.

For one thing, taken as literature, they both express an anti-evolutionary view of the future. Contemporary commercial sf fantasy almost by definition is set either in a pseudo-past or a future which has devolved to resemble a pseudo-past, in terms of its technology, attitude toward science when there is one, forms of social and political organization, and indeed even conscious-ness as expressed in the common pseudo-archaic prose style of such epics. Series novels which are not fantasy tend to be "science fantasy" because the essence of the series novel is that the familiar universe created must continue to exist within its familiar parameters for the duration of the series. Any mutational progression puissant enough to alter social, political, or psycho-logical reality will destroy the familiar consistency of the background. Since science proceeds and interacts with culture in precisely this mutational evolutionary manner, an open-ended sf series cannot be informed by what in a certain sense may be called the social esthetic of progressive science.

Taken as commercially-tailored product rather than litera-ture, series novels and fantasy are even more closely similar. They are crafted to appeal to much the same audience in terms of psychology, demographics, and marketing strategy. In commer-cial terms, they are for all practical purposes (namely maximizing income) the same thing. Indeed, fantasy novels themselves are dominantly novel series. In fact, it is possible to synthesize a commercial formula for the prodution of both without regard to specifics of their "differences."

Plot: A single heroic lead, male or female, but more often male, is propelled by special destiny on a picaresque quest across a danger-and-wonder-ridden landscape through many thrilling physical adventures toward an apotheosis that will occur only when the sales figures signal that the run of the series is at an end.

Setting: Not a unified or even multiple culture with self-awareness of all its parts and histories, but a fragmented series of subcultures alienated from each other and from meaningful, historical connection to the common human past, so that the hero may wander wide-eyed forever through the ever-changing scenery.

Characters: A male or female ingenue possessed of courage, single-valued moral innocence, physical prowess, righteousness, and a secret identity as the darling of destiny. Either a continuing love interest, one per episode, or both. A blackhearted villain corrupted by Faustian hubris.

Schtick: Rogues with hearts of gold. Fabulous cities. Treacherous wastelands. The magic of lost knowledge and forbidden civilizations. Unlikely allies. Alien creatures of both higher and lower spiritual orders. Outre flora and fauna. Desperate battles for survival against impossible odds. Wiser beings than ourselves to watch over us. Unspeakable and therefore indescribable horrors.

Commercially speaking, it cannot be denied that this commercial formula works. The bottom line proves it. The stylization of so much of the product of the sf apparatus into just this formula has so neatly coincided with the commercial boom in same that it would be hard to deny causality.

This stuff sells. It is well-tailored to the psychology of the audience for which it is targeted, it builds sales from book to book through familiarization, and I would be ill-serving the pecuniary interest of the would-be sf writers reading this column if I contended otherwise. Not only does this stuff sell, it builds you into a recognizable brand name. Not only does it build you into a brand name, it is cost-effective, being easier and quicker to write than the old-fashioned sort of sf which required the writer to reconsider the parameters of human civilization each time a new work was begun.

Which puts me into a quandary vis-a-vis this column. While I have dabbled herein in areas not entirely related to economic survival as an sf writer, I have never advocated career courses of action which I knew to be antithetical to maximizing income.

Now I am sorely tempted to do so. Lately, there have been subterranean rumblings within our little universe, stirrings of discontent, a rising feeling that something is wrong. One thing that is obviously wrong, of course, is that the peak of the boom is receding. Another thing that is wrong is the devolution of sf packaging back towards sleaze. A third obvious wrong is the invasion of sf by conglomerate media marketing thinking.

But beneath all this there seems to be something wrong with the literature itself. As witness the advent of such publications as *Venom,* dedicated to the anonymous savaging of anything within its reach, and *Patchin Review,* with its Cassandra cries of doom, sniping gossip column, and ill-focused sense of esthetic outrage.

At the risk of adding my own voice to this growing undercurrent of churlishness, I am tempted now in these pages to advise established pros and would-be sf writers alike to examine the state of their spirits as well as their bank balances, to measure their idealism against the current exigencies of the marketplace, to ask themselves *why* they are writing science fiction instead of something else, to look into their hearts as well as the Nielsens.

How foolish and naive I sound even to myself as I read these words emerging from the keyboard! How uncomfortable it feels to be voicing such sappy sentiments in public! Such saccharine idealistic considerations, such high-falutin' literary pretentiousness, such jejune supposition that the struggle and destiny of an sf writer has a parameter beyond economic triumph, such adolescent moonings over philosophical basis and esthetic intent went out with the New Wave, with Tony Boucher and John W. Campbell, with the Ace Specials and George Ernsberger, with Betty Ballantine and Michael Moorcock's *New Worlds,* with, fer chrissakes, Judy Merril, and the *first Dangerous Visions* and Jim Blish, with a ludicrous period during which argument over the style and content of science fiction, over its politics and esthetics, could arouse as much fervor as who has secured the highest advance on record.

No, in the modern context it would be a mistake to confuse would-be sf writers with these nebulosities, it might cause some to stunt the progress of their careers, to impoverish themselves in some idiotic children's crusade. The name of this column is STAYIN' ALIVE, and it would ill-serve that simple purpose to suggest that the phrase might have a double meaning.

JANUARY 1982
COLUMN 17

Well, it's the end of the calendar year, *Locus* is doing its suggested award reading list, and Charlie Brown has asked me to come up with a best of the year list of my own. In anticipation of the groans I'm hearing out there, let me quickly state that that is something I'm not going to do.

In fact, I'm not so sure how I feel about what *Charlie* is doing. On the one hand, many people complain that the *Locus* reading list, and in certain years the *Locus* awards, give one magazine too much clout with the Hugos, and admittedly the correlation is high. On the other hand, Charlie points out that his lists are long lists, that the idea is to call attention to worthy books and stories that may have been overlooked, and that if he, or someone, didn't do this, the correlation between ad hype and ad budget and awards would be even greater.

Trouble is, I believe both statements are true. And I think that for me to stick *my* two cents in would only muddy the waters further. I mean, what good would be Norman Spinrad's suggested awards reading list? I've written all these columns without reviewing specific books so as to keep this discourse an arena of our commonality rather than our rivalry, and I've tried to keep personalities and value judgments of specific works as much out of it as possible. To then sit down and rap out a list of my fave raves would be turning this column into something I don't want it to be, and that you probably don't want it to be either.

Besides, people who have sympathy with the viewpoints of this column might find themselves boring themselves on my recommendations, and people who think I'm an asshole might refuse to read anything I publically admit to liking.

Which is not to say I do not elsewhere express specific critical opinions. I reviewed books for *Destinies* for a year or so and do occasional criticism here and there. But those are *reviews*, which give the reader some idea of what the book being reviewed is about, and some idea of the critical frame of reference of the critic. It's not a simple list of books to be read at someone's say-so.

And that, I think, is the point. Charlie is right when he says he is performing a necessary function, his critics are right when they say it gives *Locus* too much clout over the Hugos, and I think I'm right when I say that the necessary function Charlie is now performing *shouldn't* be necessary.

Which was also the point of a previous column, that the critical mechanisms of the sf apparatus are not functioning properly. If they were, we wouldn't have a need for year-end lists. The year's work would have been chewed over from several well-known critical viewpoints, and whether intelligent readers agreed with any of them or not, they'd certainly have a feel for what was what.

Still, toward this end, perhaps I can supply some generalities, and since I'm really not interested in making awards or arbitrary 12-month periods any more central than they already are, I prefer to supply them in terms of simply the trends of the past year or so and how they may extend into the near future. Sf folk, after all, shouldn't be looking all the time backwards at literature over old Uncle Hugo's shoulder.

As we know, the two emergent trends of the past year or so (but with deeper roots in retrospect) were the rise of fantasy to at least co-dominance of the "sf genre" and the trend to novel series. These two trends seem to have combined with a certain malaise in the science fiction novel to produce, if we must, an awards year with no real obvious standout that can reasonably be called a science fiction novel.

Cynics might say that this had something to do with the economic slump in the sf industry, since there was less hype money being spent. If there isn't much advertising, and there isn't critical discourse to generally inform readers, and all these books are being churned out, then it's possible for almost anything to get lost in the shuffle.

At the same time, of course, *God Emperor of Dune* set all kinds of sales records, *The Number of the Beast* was black ink on a $500,000 advance, *Unicorn Tapestry* and *Timescape* did better as main-list books than they would have done as sf leaders, monster deals were still being made, and $2 million was shelled out for an unwritten novel by Carl Sagan.

In the last year or so, we passed out of what we had thought of as the Great Sf Boom and began to see that beyond the Boom there is not necessarily Bust. The Boom was in reality a phenomenon of transition. Now, at the other side of the transformation, we see a very different genre which may be in the process of coming to a stable configuration.

There is a much larger general audience for a few superstar turns at sf. *Omni* continues to post circulation figures that would make a paperback best seller, and the genre magazines continue to post monthly sales figures equivalent to decent sales for middling sf novels.

These changes are beginning to be reflected in a shifting pattern of hardcover sf publication. "Regular hardcover sf lines" are in steep decline. Dell and Berkley cancelled theirs, Harper and Row went into deeper limbo, Doubleday halved their list (and axed the top of the list at that), and Timescape also cut back.

On the other hand, sf novels have been cropping up in houses that don't have "regular hardcover sf lists." Holt. Viking. Morrow. Houghton-Mifflin.

Sf novel publishing in hardcover used to be a matter of selling 3000 to 7000 copies on a minimal budget mostly to libraries. Then came the Boom and some larger advances, some larger promotion, and a few sf novels broke out of these parameters in hardcover. At the same time, in the era of Reaganomics, library funds are a lot tighter than they were in the days of the Wicked Old Big Liberal Spenders, and the "regular sf lines" no longer have their "regular sf numbers."

In other words, in the future, sf novels are likely to be published in hardcover mostly like other kinds of hardcover novels, namely on a book by book basis. Hardcover prices are too high for schlockmeister mass marketing procedures to show much black ink here.

At the same time, however, the schlockmeister mentality is beginning to pervade the entire paperback industry and somehow seems to show profit on a flop rate of 50%. Here, instead of sf publishing getting more like mainstream pubishing, mainstream publishing has become more and more like sf genre publishing. There is no mainstream in paperback publishing any more. Everything is a genre. Every genre has stylized packaging. Ideally, every novel will be written to a different tested formula aimed at a different demographic slice. There are slime-mold operators who really see this as the wave of the future in the industry. As witness Jove's authorless generic novels, and Leisure Books' incredible announcement that they were going to do plain brown wrapper books too.

In the middle of this mess, sf doesn't look in such bad shape. Its share of the publishing industry has been permanently upped, it's now possible for an sf novel to "go all the way to the top," and, if the mail I've been getting and the conversations I've been having lately are any indication, there's a lot more idealism left here than in the middle of the larger piranha tank.

Yet, something seems missing from the literature itself lately. The genrefication of all paperback publishing has not been without its effects on sf. Surely the avalanche of sequels and series reflects this bottom-line principle of marketing, and in their own terms, the marketing boys may be right, since they've been able to flog this stuff successfully.

The shift to fantasy, I'm beginning to think, is part of a peculiarly unwholesome phenomenon in the macroculture. By now, alas, science, technology, indeed perhaps even logical deduction, have become identified in the public psyche with radiation, pollution, the military-industrial complex, and spiritual constipation. To this consciousness-style, the model of a hopeful future is a return to the less active modes of the past, to the things of the spirit which are seen as the antithesis of the scientific intellect.

These, I think, are the people who are reading all that fantasy. These are people who were probably attracted to the "sf genre" in the broadest sense by the same thing in a way that always attracted the technophiles, namely the desire to transcend the "mundane reality" of the personal present. But the technophiles seek their transcendence in a Faustian triumph of intellect over nature, whereas the technophobes seek a simpler Lost

Golden Age of Magic.

Also, of course, even less fanatical technophobes can probably still place more credence in a future transformed by science than in the return of warriors, wizards, dragons, and magic. Fantasy is a different contract with the reader than science fiction; in the former, the reader willingly suspends disbelief in the impossible, in the latter it is the writer's job to suspend the reader's disbelief by making even improbable things seem possible. Science fiction is the art of the possible, and fantasy is the art of the impossible, which I think is as close a true definition as you can get.

Unfortunately, these days the public at large is rather confused about what is impossible and what is not, between magic and science, between astrology and astronomy, between cities in space and UFOs, between lasers and pyramid power. And so we have a great deal of fantasy and science fantasy which arises out of, contributes to, and to a certain extent panders to as well, this inability of so many people to separate fantasy from science fiction.

When readers can clearly distinguish science fiction from fantasy, which is to say know when they are supposed to agree to play let's pretend and when they are to judge reality by their full perceptions, we have two very different kinds of esthetics. When you jumble them together and try to make them the same sort of thing, you get a genre formula for both based on the strengths of neither; based, more or less, on the *Star Wars* formula of sword fights and naval battles in space, of superscience intermingled with The Force, based, in other words, on the lowest common denominator between science fiction and fantasy: the adolescent power-fantasy.

It is precisely this linkage of psychic structures with product "properly designed" to fit them that is the essence of any successful "formula" for a "genre." That's what sf is in marketing terms today, an interchangeable acronym for science fiction and fantasy: voila, the "sf genre."

These dire words having been spoken, it also seems to me that we may soon be seeing the emergence of a counter-trend. The readership for fantasy, after all, didn't arise in a vacuum. Or maybe it did. Maybe it arose in the vacuum left by science fiction's general shunning of certain literary areas, reflecting perhaps the credibility gap in the country at large between the things of science and the things of the spirit.

Now by things of the spirit, I certainly don't mean magic or the supernatural. What I mean is, I suppose, what are sometimes counter-poised to sterile technocracy as the "human questions." Moral questions. Cosmological questions. Questions of fate and destiny and the nature of free will. Ambiguity. Paradox. Reflexiveness. The stuff that makes a novel of any ambitious kind more than character sketches and a plot summary, the stuff that at least opens questions of literary merit by assaying a connection between the story and the human heart.

As long as science fiction eschews dealing with things of the spirit in this quite unsuperstitious and not anti-rational sense, so long will fantasy feed the hunger for such discourse within the readership for some imaginative literature. So long as fantasy attempts to become some form of "sf," so long will fantasy tend to feed that hunger with formula plots and the moribund imagery of ancient magics.

Thus, it is not entirely impossible that something new could come out of this artificial marriage of science fiction and fantasy under the aegis of the "sf genre." In the best of all possible worlds, *two* transformed literatures would emerge out the other end—a humanized and spiritualized science fiction and a fantasy without reliance on archetypal plot-structures, stereotyped characters, or automatic imagery.

In the worst of all possible worlds, *one* literature will emerge—a denatured amalgam written according to a marketing formula, and designed to best push tender young buttons.

This being (let us hope!) neither the best nor the worst of worlds, I think we will find ourselves with both.

FEBRUARY 1982
COLUMN 18

Now although STAYIN' ALIVE was conceived as a column for writers, it has been brought to my attention that many editors (and even publishing executives, a different breed of cat) read it too; besides, one can hardly treat the life and problems of the science fiction writer indefinitely without coming up against the editorial interface. Which, in reality, is a human being with problems of his own, including a whole set of commercial, creative, psychological, and moral ambiguities.

To begin with, an editor of fiction, and a book editor in particular, is in a peculiar position. He is hired to perform several functions, not all of which are in harmony with each other.

Firstly, there is the primary function of acquisitions editor.

An editor must read submissions, reject those he doesn't want, select those he does, and establish rapport with the writers he wants to publish so that, ideally, he will get first look at most of the books he would most like to see. Even *this* breaks down into two functions which are not always in harmony—the editor must serve as Caesar giving the thumbs up or thumbs down while at the same time attracting the writers he wants to his line, discovering and developing new writers, and pursuing his literary interests. In this regard, he must achieve a general position of esteem in the eyes of the writing community, which really *is* a community in the case of sf.

But,then, secondly, he must buy the books he wants for his line, and that's where the ambiguity begins. The second function of an editor is that of buyer of books for his line, which is to say acting as negotiator on behalf of the corporation which ultimately employs him. This, of course, is when your good friend and literary comrade becomes Uncle Scrooge.

There is a peculiar machismo in this. In boom times, when editors are chasing books and writers, editorial status is enhanced both within the house and within the editorial community by the size of the advances that an editor has the power to offer, which is incidentally nice for writers. But in slacker times, editors count coup by how cheaply they can acquire books, which, of course, is not so nice for writers, and does not generally increase an editor's esteem in their eyes.

Notice the inverse power relationship here too. In a seller's market, writers and their agents take editors for as much money as they can, and first novels are easier to sell for more money, and the editor is riding high too. In boom times, when the writers have the power, editors do well too and aren't that much concerned with the greed of their suppliers, since they're only spending the money of a faceless corporation and their status in the corporate pecking order is partially determined by the size of the corporate line of credit. Everyone loves everybody in Fat City.

But when times get a little tough, and the corporate powers that be put the inevitable squeeze on, the job of the editor becomes to pass that squeeze on down to the writers, who have nowhere to pass the diminishing buck except their discontent or ire, and editors tend more to be perceived as the class enemy. When the going gets tough, the tough may get going, but when times get tough, even creampuffs get a little meaner. Nobody loves anybody in a jungle. When the corporate screws are put on, both editors and writers tend to perceive each other as adversaries.

Aside from proving that money will get you through times of no poverty better than poverty will get you through times of no money, this points to the existential core of the dilemma in which the editor is stuck.

On the one hand, an editor has to like hanging around with writers, aiding their creative process, and cultivating good relations with them, since he's going to spend most of his working time doing this, and if he doesn't enjoy it, he won't do it well. Through this process, friendships develop. Common sympathies arise. Working trust is established.

But on the other hand, an editor, and no one more than a lowly sf editor, is the economic instrument of a corporate golem, an agent of the writer's inherent economic adversary.

This dichotomy gets even more complicated when it comes to the highest editorial function, namely actually working with the writer on the tender flesh of his creation to improve the breed.

After all, no working relationship rests on more fragile ground than this. In order to presume to create a world and people to begin with, a writer must possess more than ordinary ego, and once this is done, a protective attitude toward his own deathless prose. In order to listen to someone who's telling you that *he* sees how maybe it could be better, one must believe that the editor and oneself are of like mind, are allies seeking the same agreed-upon goal. Otherwise, the editing process swiftly degenerates into a power struggle, and who has the best of the editing rights clause in the contract becomes critical.

Alas, frequently in the past, and perhaps a bit less frequently in the present, the editor becomes the conduit for corporate fiats inflicted upon the work. Such as one hardcover house telling one famous sf writer to cut 30 pages from his book, "*any* 30 pages," or the same house telling another writer to purge his novel of all "sex or politics." We all have our horror stories.

The best editor in the world under these conditions will lose all literary credibility and the confidence of his writers, and will be perceived as he has been forced to function, as a censor to be combatted.

But even without becoming the enforcer of the corporate limits which seem to be fading away over the past decade, the editor whom the writer must trust with his work is also the guy with whom the writer negotiated his last contract. Leading one writer I know to contend that "no writer has any friend on the other side of the desk." Of course, if your editor has lavished big bucks upon you, you are less likely to feel this way.

Finally, of course, the editor has to publish the book. He must, with the aid of (or in spite of) the art director and the copywriters, get the package together. He must buy ads, or, more likely, fight for an ad budget. He must pick a distribution target and motivate the salesmen into fulfilling it.

When the sales of a book do not meet the writer's expectations, the writer usually blames the incompetence of the editor. When the sales of a book do not meet the editor's expectations, he may come to blame the writer, at least when it comes to negotiating the next contract.

Actually, of course, though few editors would care to admit it, the publishing of the book is the part of the process over which the editor has least control, though, alas, it is probably the biggest cause of distrust between writer and editor. Art directors are political animals more powerful than any sf editor. Ad budgets must be cozened out of tight-fisted corporate manager types. Distribution targets are really controlled by the marketing department and are generally self-fulfilling prophecies.

Most sf editors probably detest the grinding down of this corporate machinery as much as writers do. Their loyalties are split down the middle. On the one hand, it does them no good to see fucked-up corporate procedures screwing up *their* books. On the other hand, they are being hired to front for their publishing corporation to the writers, to use bad sales figures as bargaining points in contract negotiations, and to come on like they are working for the best of all possible outfits. Also, of course, to admit to writers that books are being badly published due to factors beyond their control is to admit to an absence of power and thereby lose face.

Despite all this, the history of the sf genre, as has been often pointed out, is as much a history of editors as of writers. Papa Gernsback, who created its commercial concept, as well as some of its cheapjack practices. John W. Campbell, who midwifed the birth of the "professional sf writer," discovered the writers who formed the core of the field for two generations, and introduced speculative science as serious content. Tony Boucher, who moved the genre toward considerations of literary quality, and Horace Gold, who moved it towards the social and psychological sciences. Michael Moorcock's New Wave and Harlan Ellison's *Dangerous Visions*. Damon Knight's ORBIT series and Terry Carr's Ace Specials. George Ernsberger's books at Avon, the Ballantines, the Del Reys, Don Wolheim, David Hartwell, Jim Frenkel, etc., etc. We all know the litany. For those who know the language, the history of the genre can be read out of a recitation of mere editorial names.

Today, though, folks, there seems to be a certain decline in the esteem in which writers in general hold editors in general, a certain loss of confidence. In part, of course, this is because slack-time psychology is at work, editors have the bargaining power, and advances are no longer automatically going up. In part, too, because the corporate publishing follow-through has not been on the level of the expectations raised by advances and editorial assurances.

But I wonder if something else isn't at work here too. As the publishing industry was gobbled up by corporate media con- glomerates, so was it infused with the corporate bottom-line mentality and decision-making process. As sf boomed into greater economic significance, so was it sucked deeper into these corporate machineries. Series novels. Science fantasies. Regenre- fication. Economic determinism had its effect upon what writers were writing.

Editors, as always, served as the interface between the corporate machinery and the creative producers. More and more, they came to be judged by the bottom line themselves. As the boom slackened, the game of editorial chairs, instead of being a game of upwards and onwards became a game of keeping a place for your own ass. When editorial jobs are tight, editors are not likely to become the advocates of their writers against the commercial interface. When the bottom line becomes the Bottom Line, literary considerations become less personally important than brute survival. Vision becomes a bit blinkered by fear and paranoia.

But what all the "great editors" had is precisely some vision, cause, or goal that transcended commercial parameters. Campbell had about one a month. Tony Boucher wanted to see a literate sf. Moorcock aimed at a reinvigorating cross-fertilization between a genrefied sf and a moribund mainstream tradition. Ellison wanted to purge the genre of content and linguistic taboos. Carr and Ernsberger wanted to do for the sf novel what Boucher had done for short fiction. And so forth.

What the great editors had and what seems to now be in somewhat shorter supply is editorial idealism. Which is not to say that the current crop is a bunch of cynical villains. Rather does there seem to be a lack of idiosyncratic philosophical and literary taste on the part of most current sf editors.

I mean, you always knew what John Campbell stood for, and

if you didn't, he was more than willing to tell you. You knew what Moorcock or Ellison or Boucher considered literature and what they considered rubbish. You could read the taste of Terry Carr or George Ernsberger from what they published.

That's what I mean by an editorial idealism. An editor who possesses it has asked and answered the question, why am I doing this work? Beyond the fact that I have to make a living, why am I editing sf instead of something else? Why am I editing at all instead of selling insurance or pursuing a military career or dealing dope?

Of course everyone who has asked this question comes up with a different answer. But every editor who has answered this question for himself is operating off a center that has nothing to do with economic considerations, and every editor who hasn't even asked himself this question is operating off a void, and therefore tends to become an economically-determined extension of the corporate machinery.

The outward extension of inward idealistic esthetics is courage. A writer operating off such a center will have the courage to defend the meaning and integrity of his work against the pressures of the commercial interface, though, hopefully, not to a suicidal absolute. An editor operating off such a center will also have a courage born of the knowledge that his lifework is contributing to something with more meaning in an absolute sense than the sacred bottom line. Such an editor is entitled to think of himself as engaged in genuine creative activity and to receive the respect of writers as such.

Which is not to say that any editor can sanely and safely afford to become the writer's champion against the corporate establishment or ignore the economic imperatives of the market-place. But if your compromises in the name of survival are also compromises in the service of some self-chosen higher goal, then they remain pragmatic means to that end, and do not end up becoming your *raison d'etre* itself.

Since editors known for their literary dedications tend to attract like-minded authors, since authors who can choose editors instead of the reverse tend to be the most desirable to publish, and since readers ultimately tend to prefer works conceived and executed with some genuine passion to machine-made product, in the long run, a sense of editorial idealism is probably good business too.

MARCH 1982
COLUMN 19

Having, over the past few months' worth of columns, come to the perception that the "Sf Boom," rather than being a swing of the old sine curve, was a phenomenon marking a series of transformations, both esthetic and economic, and having explored the nature of the new environment to a degree, we now, of course, must ask ourselves what we are going to do about it in terms of career strategies.

Before a writer considers career strategy, he must first, of course, consider career goal, which is to say, what do you want to be when you grow up? Obviously the beginning writer reading this column at least thinks he knows the answer. He wants to grow up to be a successful science fiction writer. Otherwise, why read this stuff, or buy *Locus* in the first place? But this may not be as simple as it sounds, especially in the 1980s.

Indeed, in the 1970s, a number of "successful science fiction writers" in mid or even peak career decided, at least temporarily, that they *hadn't* become what they wanted to be when they grew up, or that they hadn't really grown up at all, or that they couldn't mature further as "science fiction" writers, and they announced that they were "leaving science fiction" for the greener pastures of the mainstream, or even retiring from writing altogether.

Now, of course, these diverse writers had diverse reasons and goals, but they all (or should I say *we* all) had certain conceptions in common. None of us, I think, really wanted to radically change the stuff we were writing, to eschew speculative content and deal mimetically with the here and now, although I, at least, wanted, and still want to deal with the here and now mimetically from time to time. One way or another, the idea was to get rid of the "sf" label, to break into the "mainstream," to be "taken more seriously," and, of course, to make lots more money.

In other words, the impulse to leave "sf" for "mainstream" had little to do with dissatisfaction with the work itself and everything to do with how the work was received—critically, popularly, and economically.

In those days, "mainstream" was perceived as synonymous with "big league." Vonnegut was "mainstream." Ditto Bradbury. Towards the end of the 1970s, Stanislaw Lem "broke through into mainstream." Likewise Ursula LeGuin.

Mainstream was "serious literature." Mainstream was the "general novel." Mainstream was respectable hardcover publication with respectable covers, reviews in the *New York Times*

Book Review & Co. Mainstream was the possibility of big advances, big sales, fame, fortune, and the Johnny Carson Show. Mainstream, in short, was perceived as the Big World Out There. Making it in the mainstream was perceived as making the jump from Triple A to the Majors, becoming a real, serious, adult writer. Mainstream was perceived as the opposite of "sf," a genre targeted at adolescents, in which sales were limited, serious literary work not seriously valued, and literary growth beyond a certain modest point impossible.

Between 1969 and 1977, I wrote three "mainstream" novels. They suffered diverse fates. But what they all had in common was that they were "genreless." However successful they were or weren't literarily or commercially, they were written off high literary intent. Which is not to say I wasn't lusting after bigger bucks; rather my perception was that if one wrote a good novel that ignored and transcended genre parameters, a "general novel" of excellence, one would then be "breaking into the mainstream." And I believe that most of the writers who were agonizing over "sf versus mainstream" at the time were similarly motivated.

Today, some quite successful "sf writers" are more quietly talking about "breaking out of the genre" again. But this time the talk is different. One *very* successful sf writer has told me that he wants to move in the direction of "the Stephen King kind of contemporary horror novel." Another is determined to make a big rep as a "fantasist." Another is writing "romances" under a pseudonym. I myself am trying to market an outline for what my agent insists must be dubbed a "thriller."

With different degrees of self-awareness, perhaps, we all recognize that the "mainstream" some of us were trying to "break into" earlier no longer exists. The general novel no longer exists. Which is to say that no novel can successfully be marketed simply as a "novel." In the 1980s, "mainstream" has become a mosaic of genre categories: thrillers, historical romances, mysteries, contemporary romances, literary novels, women's novels, etc., etc. ad nauseam. Each genre of "mainstream" has its own recognizable packaging, its own characteristic marketing patterns, its own A and B books, its own overlay of commercial constraints and genre formula, its own allocation of rack slots.

Including sf. In this sense, sf *has* succeeded in merging with the mainstream. It is another part of the mainstream mosaic. It is now possible for sf novels to garner large advances and big sales, just like romances, literary novels, or thrillers. The spread between the bottom and the top in the sf genre is now about the same as the spread in other genres of mainstream. How an sf novel will now do is as much a matter of self-fulfilling marketing and packaging strategy as is the fate of mysteries, thrillers, or women's novels. The publishing industry now perceives its total market as a series of demographic slices, each one with a genre aimed at capturing it. Saturate any one of them, including the sf slice, and you have a best seller. Try to be all these things to all readers, which is to say, write a general novel of excellence with no genre marketing potential, and you are nowhere.

So where does this leave the question of career strategy for the "sf writer" or, more broadly, the writer with the esthetic impulse to write speculative fiction?

It depends, of course, on your ultimate goal. First, let us assume that the ultimate goal is to make as much money as possible, period. Let us also assume a very high level of skill and perfect cynicism. While it is now possible to reach the level of best-sellerdom by saturating the sf slice of the demographic pie (the *Dune* series, Robert Heinlein, *Ringworld Engineers*, etc.), it is a smaller demographic slice than most, meaning that the odds against achieving such saturation are high, and few sf novels a year will make it. You'd probably be better off edging into "thrillers" (a sub-genre of which deals with a kind of near-future sf) or the "Stephen King-type contemporary horror genre," both of which appeal to larger demographic slices, which means you can reach best seller levels without needing total saturation, which means that more books per annum achieve this status, which means, other things being equal, that your odds are better.

Often this is entirely a matter of marketing strategy, and not the intrinsic nature of the book. Many "Stephen King-type horror novels" are packaged as "sf" and sell like sf. *Vampire Tapestry* did better as a middle-list contemporary horror novel than it could have as an "sf leader." Any number of successful "thrillers" have as much speculative element as certain sf novels which they have greatly outsold. In general, if you can shift your work into one of these other genres, you will make more money. Provided, of course, that it is published as an "A" book and not a "B."

Which, of course, is the Catch-22. A money-hungry writer possessed of skill and cynicism at the outset of his career is probably better off moving in this direction. But an established "sf name" trying to shift genre is probably going to be published as a "B" writer at least at first, since clout simply doesn't seem to carry over into a neighboring demographic slice of the mainstream. So, if you are an sf "name" with clout, and again assuming cynicism, greed, and skill, you'd probably be better off in "sf."

The strategy here must be to do books that will saturate the smaller sf market. Given the right product and sufficient clout, you can have your work published as an "A" sf novel these days. Meaning packaged quite differently from the regular sf line, with a higher distribution target, and more advertising. Since what is necessary is the saturation of the sf market, what is needed is work that appeals to the lowest common denominator of that market. Namely a picaresque quest novel keyed into adolescent estrangement and power fantasies and cinematic sense of wonder; in other words, as perfect a fulfillment as possible of the "sf genre formula." Preferably a series, of course, which will build sales from book to book and allow the publisher to amortize an advertising and promotion budget over several novels.

These should be the alternative career strategies of the speculative writer whose ultimate goal is strictly riches, un-hampered by literary ambitions or idealism.

But what if we assume another ultimate goal? What if you want to be as free as possible to follow your literary star where it will take you, to explore the possibilities of the material itself, to push back the frontiers of the possible, to expand your own spirit and the readers' in the process, without, of course, ending up in the poorhouse in the bargain?

Not so long ago, this was the sort of "sf writer" who longed to "break into mainstream" and perhaps schemed and fought to achieve that Ultima Thule. "Mainstream" was the place where you could get larger advances, develop a larger audience, secure critical attention, and be free of the taboos, formulas, and perception of the readership as adolescents of the "sf genre."

But that "mainstream" no longer exists.

Becoming a "mainstream writer" is no longer a viable career strategy. The few "mainstream superstars" are their own genre and achieved that status before the transformation of "main-stream" into a genre mosaic. Starting out today, they would probably end up either as "mass market best seller writers" ignored by the critics of "serious literature" or "serious literary writers" published in small hardcover editions and scrambling for any paperback sale at all, and they would have to make career decisions as to which they wanted to grow up to be early on.

Today, the question is, *which* genre of the mainstream offers the best compromise between literary freedom, idealism, ability to publish experimental and frontier-pushing work, and eco-nomic well-being?

For the moment, at least, the answer seems to be science fiction.

Assuming a certain level of excellence—high enough at least to sell maybe one monthly leader a year at worst for a median advance—the science fiction writer may be forced to settle for lumpfish caviar and California champagne, but at least it is still caviar and champagne, and not red beans and rice with Ripple. Let's say it takes you six months to do a novel, the advance is say $15,000, which is not out of line, foreign rights get you another $10,000, and you have six months a year to do other work, which, as an sf writer, can be short stories you can actually sell. If you can't survive on that, then maybe your ultimate goal is riches and you should rethink your priorities.

As an sf writer on this economic level, you don't have to do lowest common denominator work aimed at saturating the sf market. You can even spend half your time experimenting with short stories if you want to, which is not something a writer in the other genres of mainstream can afford to do. At this economic level, assuming a reasonable degree of excellence, you can write and publish fiction closer to your heart than to some marketing maven's genre formula.

And, of course, in the current market, you still *do* have the possibility at least of striking it rich with science fiction. You could get lucky. Or you could win an award and be in a bargaining position to force publishers to compete for your next book and publish it in an "A" manner.

Indeed, if you *are* struck by greed, you can design yourself a lowest-common-denominator sf novel series, be pretty much assured of at least selling it, and have a shot at breaking through to more exalted economic levels.

At which point, you will be in an interesting position. You will have a flush bank account. You will be under pressure to do more of the same. But if you have your head screwed on straight, you won't have to.

An sf writer of my acquaintance achieved large commercial success with an sf novel with a one-word title. "Young man," he was told by a high publishing executive after turning in his next book with a multi-word title, "from now on, you must have one-word titles on all of your books."

There the anecdote as told to me ends. But I know what I would have told that worthy.

I woulda said, "You've got two things wrong. First of all, it's

Mr. Spinrad to you, Charlie. Second of all, you know what a best-selling science fiction writer sells next? Anything he wants to."

PART SIX
HOW THINGS WORK

Unlike the rest of this book, this valedictory essay is not being written as a column to a monthly deadline; rather it is an attempt to put the evolutionary process of the columns into some kind of overall perspective. Since this *is* a book by someone who openly admits he is primarily a science fiction writer, it might as well be a science fictional perspective.

And in the process of writing these columns over evolutionary time, I think that one thing I've discovered is that there *is* such a thing as a science fictional perspective on reality, a dialectic that can be applied to such sublimities as the production of visionary art and such practicalities as negotiating a book contract. What this science fictional perspective really is, of course, is a question as unanswerable as "how do you define science fiction?" But I think at root it has something to do with wanting to know how things work.

How things *really* work, not how some authority figure tells you they work; not the rules of the game, but the game behind the rules. The straight poop, the inside story.

Kids who grow up to be scientists, science fiction writers, or investigative journalists, all start out wanting to know how things really work. The scientist wants to know how material reality works, the investigative reporter's ideal is a knowledge of the fine detail of social politics with scientific precision, and the science fiction writer would like to know how both of these realities affect the individual reality of consciousness.

The science fiction writer would like to know this because

more often than not he's writing stories set in a future. Since he's writing about a world as yet unknown to either scientific verification or efficient muckraking reporters, he's got to imagine how imaginary changes in social or scientific reality affect imaginary characters. In order to do this with some coherence, he needs a general theory of how things really work.

And the only place he can derive it from is the passage of his own consciousness through reality. So the science fiction writer tends to have the scientist's curiosity about the way physical and cultural mechanisms work, and the reporter's scepticism about the moral perfection of authority.

Maybe that explains why there is such a magazine as *Locus*, why SFWA is both internally contentious and externally militant, and why I wrote this book.

Re-reading these columns, it seems to me that the basic thrust of all of them has been to investigate how things really work in the art and commerce of publishing.

In another sense, the columns have been a kind of science fiction about publishing, a description of a cultural mechanism and the interaction of its grindings with the art of science fiction. That's material for a science fiction novel, isn't it? At least one has been written, Barry Malzberg's *Herovit's World*.

No doubt there are some people who will consider such obsession with the straight poop to have a paranoid component. Learned professors have written treatises on the paranoid component of science fiction. Dr. Strangelove and Dr. Frankenstein are the most prevalent images of science. Reporters are obsessed with discovering evil forces everywhere.

On the other hand, it could be argued that evil forces *do* exist wherever there is power, that scientific descriptions of reality trouble the spirit, and that the universe really is out to get us, or worse, is entirely indifferent to our destiny.

Certainly science fiction writers have ample evidence to support the theory that sinister forces are against us. It is plain fact that the literature of science fiction has been walled up in a critical and commercial ghetto for the better part of half a century. In our struggles to breach the wall, though, we have perhaps sometimes lost our science fictional perspective. Or, as Theodore Sturgeon puts it, forgotten to ask the next question.

Which is *why*.

Why is science fiction considered beyond the sphere of discourse of the New York Literary Establishment? *Why* has it been genrefied for 50 years under commercial pressure towards a product marketed to juveniles and away from adults?

Why has this persisted for nearly half a century?

There are those who will argue from a genetic perspective that this situation evolved from an unfortunate chance mutation. When Hugo Gernsback coined the logo "scientification" for a new magazine in 1926, he was, in a sense, inventing the science fiction genre as a sub-genre of the boy's adventure story. This created a popular mass culture market for a genre that had never before existed as a formula for commercial fiction. That new formula was circumscribed by the general genre parameters of the boy's adventure story. It was a new market. It attracted formula commercial writers. It created a certain image of science fiction, later reinforced by the emergence of science fiction fandom.

By now we all know what that image is. So we can see why it repelled writers who considered themselves to have serious literary ambition. The image became self-fulfilling. Once an image becomes self-fulfilling, it affects reality. And an image powerful enough to alter the reality it epitomizes is bound to be very stable. In a sense, it defends its own existence. Which explains why the public perception of science fiction has until recently remained static through all the evolutionary changes of the past half century. Once the literature of science fiction was epitomized by a genre image as juvenile cult material, all literature in this mode was ghettoized behind that image and not subject to ongoing critical attention from the culture at large. A chance mutation had carved out an ecological niche and then been adapted by natural selection to fit its parameters.

But Sturgeon would still probably insist that we ask the next question. The mutation might have been random, but the fact that it proved viable, the fact that it ended up being selected for, must have been due to the cultural environment. It must have had a cultural *reason* to exist.

At which point, we must descend from lofty scientific metaphor into down and dirty pragmatics.

Which brings us right back to how things really work.

I mean, look at the 50 years or so during which science fiction has been a ghettoized genre. Passingly strange. Radio! Television! A world-wide economic depression! Larger than life maniacs in power in Italy, the Soviet Union, and Germany! A World War! The Atomic Bomb! The Cold War! The Cuban Missile Crisis! The Space Race! The Assassination of JFK! The Sexual Revolution! The Rock Revolution! Viet Nam! The Moon Landing! Transistors! Microchips! Hand-held computers! TV from Jupiter and Saturn!

Is this not the material of science fiction? Can a literature dealing with this material be anything *but* central to the cultural life of the United States in the 20th Century?

Apparently so.

But not without cost.

Which brings us back to where we are now.

We *do* know where we are now, don't we? We're in the United States of America on the planet Earth, pushing, you should pardon the cliche, 1984. We don't seem to understand how to make our modern industrial economy work any more. It can't be because our technological level is declining. We're capable of launching space shuttles and creating designer genes. It isn't because we've lost the cutting edge of pure science; our understanding of the physical parameters of reality has never been more sophisticated and comprehensive.

Our economic level has been declining, in that, in national and individual terms, we're poorer than we were, and this as-yet-but-dimly-perceived devolution in standard of living has already sapped the national spirit of its confidence in the upward evolution of our civilization.

Or maybe it's the other way around.

After all, we haven't lost a bit of scientific knowledge or technological technique. It can't even be said we know less about economics than our ancestors.

On the other hand, we *do* find ourselves in a society where science has become identified with radiation, cancer, and militarism, where reason itself is regarded with suspicion as the product of the uptight half of the brain, where the teaching of "creation science" has become a serious political issue.

While our arch-competitor, ex-protege, and wistful current role model, Japan, happily relates to its robots as creatures native to a technological environment.

What we've lost that the Japanese seem to have is confidence in a positive ongoing evolution of civilization in a cultural and spiritual sense through science and technology. In the United States, it's become almost embarrassing to suggest in public the possibility that ongoing progressive and enthusiastic development of science and technology is a necessary life-sign of an economically and psychically healthy civilization.

What we've got that the Japanese don't have is a deeply perceived dichotomy in our society between reason and feeling, between logic and emotion, between the things of the spirit and the things of science.

140

We can barely form the concept that *science itself* is a thing of the spirit and that "things of the spirit" do not mean magic and the supernatural.

We tend to confuse the scientific method, which is a careful and obsessively objective *means* for verifying insights into the nature of physical reality, and the scientific impulse, which is the spiritual *end*, the emotional goal behind all this cold analysis. Namely the lust to know how things really work. How *all* things really work, from the ultimate constituents of matter to the ultimate knowledge of the universe itself as a synergetic system, to total comprehension of the phenomenon of consciousness itself. One may question the hubris of this transcendent millennial Faustian quest, but hardly the human emotion and visionary longing that motivate it in spiritual terms.

We also tend to confuse screwed-up or imperfect technology with baseness in the goal of technological development. Which, of course, is to use the best current knowledge of how things really work to figure out how to make them work better. Technology will *never* be perfect until both our knowledge of the universe and our use of it are perfect. Judging from our present state, we can assume that we still have a long way to go.

But maybe we can't assume that we're going to get there. Lately we've begun to confuse science with magic, energy with metaphor, the things of the spirit with supernatural forces, how things really work with how we would like them to work. When an individual confuses how things really work with how he would like them to work—when he runs into a wall in the sublime assurance that his will will allow him to walk through it—we say he is psychotic. When a culture begins to disregard the parameters of reality, we can only call it a crisis of civilization.

The crisis is neither entirely scientific nor entirely spiritual, for it is precisely a crisis in the *interface* between the things of science and the things of the spirit, between the individual consciousness and the total social and material surround.

This, of course, is also precisely what most science fiction is about, when it is about anything but a rehashing of a basic formula plot skeleton.

Any culture which relegates this central discourse to a genre ghetto in order to dismiss it as trivial is in deep shit, because science fiction's sphere of discourse is anything but trivial to the crisis confronting progressive technological and scientific man.

Just how trivial it isn't can be read easily enough by the consequences of its absence from our civilization's main intellectual marketplace. Where a culturally central literature of science fiction should stand, we have a stunted creature shoehorned into a commercial formula and struggling to maintain its integrity. We also have a literature of the impossible donning "sf" drag and pretending to be mimetic, itself the creation of the sf genre formula. Coincidentally, in the society itself, we also have a growing confusion of science and fantasy, a schizoid chasm growing between the things of science and the things of spirit, and a deadly Cartesian fallacy that they are antithetical.

We lack not only culturally central science fiction, but a cultural worldview that at least attempts to synergize scientific knowledge with the spiritual world of the individual consciousness, human goals and desires with technological power. One that at least attempts to base its perspective of how-it-would-like-things-to-work in how-things-really-work. One that applies the test of reason to things of the spirit, and applies the test of the spirit to what man might do with knowledge and power.

While we have been living through what is in essence a fifty year science fiction novel ourselves, our "serious literature" has been moving further and further from any perspective close to this; and our popular literature, indeed our popular culture, has been moving further and further toward empty format, toward what Michael Moorcock called in the very title of a science fiction novel *The Condition of Muzak*.

Within the ghetto walls, it has always been a struggle to prevent the literature of science fiction from being reduced to the Condition of Muzak. Yet somehow the literature never became entirely genrefied into mental background music. Granted, a great ream of such stuff is produced every year, but at least it can still be more or less said that there isn't much good science fiction that goes unpublished because of excessive literary ambition. And that such books more or less still regularly emerge from the wall of noise.

But for the most part, these works have not passed into the general stream of the culture. Which thus has a void in what should be a central sphere of intellectual discourse. The results of which are all too visible today.

All the more visible because what the American publishing industry and the American literary establishment caused to happen to science fiction in the past is now happening to fiction, period.

Aside from science fiction, there are a few other small areas of discourse which mainstream publishing, which is to say contemporary corporate committee conglomerate publishing, is keeping in cultural purdah. Fiction exploring the effects of drugs on our civilization. Anything set in the counter-culture of the 1960s. Anything centrally about Viet Nam, although that may be slowly changing.

Four central areas of concern, wouldn't you say, for a struggling society trying to figure out where it is, how it got there, and what to do next?

When a society starts developing multiple blind spots of *this* magnitude, it's already in a devolutionary state, and it's only a matter of time before the next stage begins to take hold: Popular literature (in the extended sense including all media purveying fiction) begins to degenerate into a mosaic of stylized genres where the format *is* the story, where the formula *is* the content, where the plot is a Skinnerian mechanism, and where all episodes are interchangeable.

Soon fiction itself ceases to become an arena of discourse for exploration of the relationship between the individual and external reality. In a sense, it *becomes* the relationship between citizen and social mechanism. It becomes an agent of the social mechanism instead of an inquiry into it. It becomes entertainment. It becomes show business.

Show. Business. Show business. People in show business are in the business of putting on a show. The purpose of putting on a show is to make money. The show that attracts the most customers will make the most money. Therefore one studies the demographics. What kind of show attracts which consumers? What imagery can we key into that is already implanted in the mass consciousness? What plot sequences exert the maximum appeal? What story elements build audience loyalty? What's the best identification figure to use?

You will note that this is exactly the sort of study that is done before a major television commercial is made. Maybe that's where the process started. Commercials are designed to sell a product, not speak to the mind or the spirit. They use all the techniques of art but they are not art because they have no artistic goal. But they taught network television how to design a product to sell. Today, episodic television, the form which utterly dominates the media-sphere, is in effect an endless series of commercials for itself.

This is what it means to quite literally produce a genre. When you have the results of your study, you then design a format around the targeted audience's psychological profile designed to sell the format itself as the product, and hire some writers to do episodes.

Once you've genrefied enough formats, you've got the total mass audience neatly cut up into demographic slices, each one with a stylized format designed to push its particular buttons, just like a good TV commercial campaign. If you've figured out the buttons right, the audience will be led through a psychologically pleasurable experience, and you will have achieved your goal—success in the Nielsens. And maximum profits.

Now that so much of publishing has become just another arm of the media conglomerates, this sophisticated bottom-line approach to selling a product has reached into the more conservative print media.

Even publishers have begun to realize that a sound, conservative but sophisticated corporate approach to selling fiction is a lot more sound bottom-line-wise than depending on the inspiration of creative talent for your fortune. If the psychological profile of the targeted audience indicates a libidinal charge on physical fear, give them physical jeopardy. If they're fantasizing violence, give them knife-flicks and gore. If it's power, give them magic. If its S&M, there are any number of image systems which will allow them to get off on it without raising them to guilty self-knowledge. Even if it's love, you can genrefy the sequences into romance.

As long as you lead the audience by the back-brain along a skein of events keyed to evoke the primal emotions like lust, hate, fear, terror, horrification, and blood-lust, you don't have to worry very much about the individual episode or book because you've got the selling format down pat.

Now all this started out being a discussion of the pragmatics of publishing from a science fictional perspective, from an obsession with how things really work, but when you finally do find out how the interface of commerce and art works, you do not end up in Kansas.

Writer or editor, you can hardly be in the business of publishing without encountering moral confrontations with the bottom line. The American publishing industry is moving toward the Condition of Muzak with unseemly rapidity. Is this because the people in charge are black-hearted villains out to rot the brains of the nation?

Not necessarily.

First of all, where you *do* find a human being still in charge of making decisions, you'll find at worst someone mindlessly serving the Sacred Bottom Line, and at best someone with a fancy title who is himself struggling with the mechanism.

Because, second of all, *people* are not exactly in charge of publishing any more. The mechanism itself is in charge. Have we been secretly conquered by an alien life-form? In a way we have, though this golem is strictly of our own creation. It's called the corporate decision-making process.

Now in a general way, the corporate decision-making process isn't such a bad idea. Instead of President Napoleon deciding everything out of his hip pocket, decisions are made by committees which not even the Chief Officer can overide by act of will. This makes policy consistent and predictable. It allows sophisticated market research to input on production plans. It prevents unsaleable goods from being turned out on someone's whim. It minimizes fuck-ups.

This is all very well when you're mass producing cars or television sets or widgets. These are ethically neutral technological artifacts.

But when you're producing *cultural* artifacts that interact with the psyche of the consumer, the corporate decision-making process turns into Frankenstein's monster.

Because it is, after all, a dead mechanism, a literal golem. It has no moral sense. It lacks a will. It just follows the program. It *is* the program.

The corporate decision-making process is programmed to maximize profit and minimize loss, which is a reasonable prime directive on which to base a business. The modern corporate program has a huge data-feed from marketing research. It also has access to all the marketing experts it needs. It has precise demographic information on its targeted consumers and sophisticated means with which to zap them. Therefore, dutifully programmed creature that it is, it follows the prime directive with utter zeal, and uses all means at its disposal to maximize the bottom line.

The horrible thing about the corporate genrefication of American publishing is that no human villains are responsible. The mechanism is responsible because the mechanism is in charge. But the mechanism has no sense of morality or esthetics. Right on the interface between commerce and art, between utter bottom-line commercial logic and the things of the spirit, we find not human beings wrestling with the inherent ambiguities but an inappropriate decision-making mechanism running out of control.

This is exactly how it is possible for a sophisticated technological society to develop huge cultural blindspots in areas of central cultural concern. The more sophisticated and complex a culture gets, the more things tend to get turned over to homeostatic decision-making mechanisms. Mechanisms which are programmed to follow some simple prime directive, but which are not programmed to judge its appropriateness. All it takes is for one of these mechanisms to be really badly placed, and almost anything can happen, against all human reason.

Which begins to explain how it was possible for the sphere of discourse of science fiction to be consigned to purdah through a half century of rapid evolutionary change during which it should have been a central cultural concern.

When Gernsback genrefied "scientification" as a sub-genre of pulp adventure fiction, a fundamental misperception was perpetrated which has dogged American science fiction ever since. While a genre format can be overlayed on science fiction to produce a commercial genre like westerns or romances or gothics, science fiction cannot be *defined* by a format. Westerns and historical genres are defined by their settings. Detective fiction is defined by its plot. Modern romances are defined by their archetypical character relationships.

But science fiction cannot be defined along any of these parameters. It isn't a place, it isn't a time, it isn't a plot, it isn't its characters. It is inherently different from everything else that has become genrefied. It confuses the mechanism. It does not compute.

Science fiction never really fit its genre parameters because no genre parameters could define it. It never really belonged as a sub-genre of boy's pulp adventure. Prior to Gernsback, science fiction existed as an occasional strange novel published and considered like any other novel. Twain and Shelley and Wells and Verne. Certainly not enough people for a real SFWA party.

But since science fiction had entered the arena of commercial genre publishing it was genrefied all the same, if not entirely as a literature, certainly in a marketing sense. When book publishers began doing science fiction, they took their packaging motifs from the pulp magazines. Not surprising then that science fiction looked like pulp genre, literally perceived as such on the racks.

Now in a properly functioning literate society, there would be a critical community capable of insight into such a malfunction and having the cultural clout to get it repaired.

But there has been an even worse malfunction in the overall

critical community itself, far-ranging, multiplex, and not born yesterday.

Until the development of mass printing, about the early 19th Century say, there was obviously no such thing as "popular literature." By modern standards, very few books were published, and in small printings, and reading was entirely an elite taste.

Then, of course, publishing became a mass market business, magazines were invented, literacy became general, and all sorts of genre formulas were concocted to appeal to the "low brows." The "high brow" literary culture, the writing and critical community in England first confronted with this cultural revolution, needed to develop some mechanism for separating the wheat from the chaff.

When books were relatively few and far between, each one could be an event in the little world of letters, but when mass publishing came in, it became necessary to apply categorical exclusions from the sphere of critical attention, or be swamped by the slushpile. Thus the pragmatic ancestors of Leavis' ossified Great Tradition and the present-day mandarinate of letters.

For of course, the moment "high brow literature" self-consciously split itself off from the genres of "low brow" commercial literature, it was on the way to genrefying *itself*.

Hadn't it already identified the targeted market and defined its parameters? Hadn't it already created a visible influence establishment to be the object of PR courtship?

For a long time now, of course, publishers have known where to advertise "high brow lit," how much to spend on it, how many books you can expect to sell, and the politics of securing reviews in the right places.

When a group of writers and critics start talking about a "Great Tradition," it is not likely they are talking about the tradition of other than their own tribe. Like the Academie Francaise, they become a self-defined elite genre. Everything not included in the genre is excluded from the tribal sphere of discourse. Instead of a Rome to which all roads lead, it bcomes a stone fortress besieged by subliterate barbarians. It becomes exclusionary. It seals itself off.

As soon as it does so, of course, it becomes fair game for the marketers. They know exactly how many copies this genre will sell—and the numbers ain't too terrific—how important it is in the balance sheet.

And so you have the present situation. "Higher Criticism,"

written by critics other critics would like to grow up to be, is ascended to babble. It becomes more and more Talmudic. It becomes more and more about its own theories and less and less about any primary object of discourse, which is to say a work of fiction. It's published in obscure journals but nevertheless it's good enough to make its creators academic superstars.

Unfortunately, the fiction in this country that calls itself avant-garde is publishing in tiny editions for little or no advances by small presses, and usually never sees a mass market edition. Which is to say it sells zilch. Which is not so surprising, seeing as it's targeted at a miniscule audience of mandarins.

Of course, by now "*mainstream* serious literature" is quite a separate genre from "*non-commercial* serious literature," and its demographics look a bit better. Here you have the power base of the New York Literary Establishment, which is to say the commercial high-brow critics and their favored writers. You can sell books in this genre. The critics are still reviewing books. They're excerptable for good jacket quotes. There are publications well-targeted to the audience in which to buy ad space. PR access to the electronic media is relatively good. You can even break a best seller out of this genre from time to time.

What is lacking in all this, of course, is any critical overview of the entire culture. Where culture lacks a critical overview, uncritical and unself-conscious mechanisms will begin to control more and more decision-making processes. And, of course, the more decision-making is given over to unself-conscious processes, the less chance there is for a critical overview to develop.

Instead, blind spots develop. Science fiction is removed from the sphere of cultural discourse. Higher criticism loses contact with reality. Academe loses contact with creative artists. Publishers lose control of their distribution. Areas of occlusion spread. A generation gap opens up. "Science" and "feeling" become dichotomized. No one seems to know how to make the economic mechanism work. Popular culture visibly declines into episodic Muzak. Alienation increases. Crime increases. New religions spring up. Things fall apart, the center cannot hold.

Because there is *nothing* at the center. No critical overview. No viewpoint that transcends the mechanism. Only a steadily increasing mindless entropy, as a civilization's destiny is taken out of the hands of the human spirit and given over to decision-making social mechanisms.

This, of course, has happened to almost all civilizations thus far to emerge on the planet Earth.

All pre-industrial civilizations achieved long-term stability by multiplying their homeostatic decision-making mechanisms to the point where even the inner life of the individual was ritualized by his role in a social mechanism programmed with theocratic absolutes.

The stability of perfect adaptation to an historical ecological niche.

But when the historical environment changes, ancient civilizations that have existed in sublime stability for centuries are overrun by industrial man. That's why they were pre-industrial civilizations, and that's what "post-industrial civilization," should we sink to that state, will be like.

Without overviews that look beyond the mechanism, without conscious awareness of culture creating itself, without a progressive evolutionary perspective, a civilization can hardly be expected to evolve progressively. The scientific method is such an overview, and what we sometimes call "Western civilization" was not the only one to evolve it. But "Western civilization" was the only one to use its knowledge of how things work to create an exponentially-evolving technology. Indeed, "Western civilization," including as it does pieces of Africa, the Middle East, the Soviet Union, and Japan—and we generally understand what we mean when we say that—consists precisely of those nations which have acquired sophisticated science and progressively evolving technology and truly integrated them into their culture.

"Western civilization" is really "technological civilization," not a geographically-distributed culture, but the current dominant stage of overall human evolution.

If we are lucky, it will prove to be an evolutionary step further toward planetary and trans-planetary civilization adapted to mastery of the evolutionary processes themselves.

If we are really too far gone along our current vector, as some would contend, we could go the way of the Romans, Manchus, Aztecs, and dinosaurs.

Just like a science fictional perspective to pursue an obsession with how things really work into a doomsday scenario!

But science fiction is or should be another overview beyond the social mechanism, another attempt to ruthlessly elucidate how things *really* work. And when it adopts the doomsday mode, the intent is to create a self-cancelling prophecy. Whether that prophecy be of totalitarian thought control, nuclear destruction, a new dark age, or the decline of intelligent and idealistically committed publishing. In a weird way, the doomsday scenarios are relentlessly progressive—the poeple who write them are proceeding from the assumption that pitfalls in the road ahead can be avoided if we can envision them.

Indeed, one of the cultural functions science fiction should have been performing more centrally all along is that of generating self-cancelling prophecies, of keeping society alert to possible pits in the road up ahead.

But an even more central cultural vacuum is the progressive evolutionary overview that should be science fiction's higher cultural function: namely to evoke visionary possible futures toward which the spirit could aspire, visions at least theoretically capable of being realized.

After all, where else are we going to get visionary images of our evolving possible futures? If science fiction isn't performing this social function, then *fiction* isn't, period.

And what we are left with are the statistical bureaucratic least-surprise images of the futurologists, devoid of the art that connects prediction to the life of the spirit. Or images from the past served up by prophets and preachers and gurus, filled with concern for the things of the spirit, but devoid of a connection to the possibility of ongoing progressive evolution. Or the future strictly as hardware from the frontiers of technology.

Science fiction really is a unique perspective on the future, in the sense that nothing else can perform its higher function. It is, ideally, fictional art informed by the visionary scientific spirit, a poetry of imagery derived from the imagination but constrained by the best available knowledge of how things really work.

As such, of course, it isn't *a* perspective on *the* future, but a multiplicity of perspectives on a multiplicity of futures. Aside from everything else, it redefines the relationship of the individual psyche to the future by creating a concept of the future as something we create by our actions in the present, as something we have a say in choosing, as an ongoing upward, consciously evolving process, as destiny rather than fate.

This is a perspective that is not addressed by fantasy or the "contemporary novel" or any other form of fiction except science fiction. Because this perspective is a functional definition of science fiction itself.

Of course, science fiction itself is full of the opposite; dire warnings of inevitable human surrender to blind ritual, of robots or computers taking over, of the degeneration of civilization, of the ultimate descent to cultural hive-mind where autonomous human consciousness no longer exists.

What science fiction really is all about in the end is both sides of the coin, the struggle within our own nature, the dialectics of human destiny.

When these matters are discussed only within a minor genre literature, they might as well not be considered at all as far as the society at large is concerned. The results we see all around us—a society that seems unable to form a positive image of an achievable progressive, evolutionary future, or at least not one in sync enough with the way things really work to be viable as a *possible* future. A society on the very threshold of an inter-planetary age which cannot make a planetary economy work. A society which has lost its confidence in social and technological evolution, which is beginning to lose the distinction between science and magic, and which is beginning to consider reason itself suspect.

But science fiction, ghettoized though it be, still exists, and with a strange grass-roots vitality. No one supports it with grants. Science fiction writers for the most part don't get to ride the literary lecture circuit or do the Johnny Carson Show. National publications don't shower science fiction with publicity. The Literary Establishment ignores it. Yet there it is, with something like 15% of the fiction market.

Maybe people aren't as dumb as blind social mechanisms. Maybe they're not even as dumb as their demographic profiles. While the elite avant-garde became foundation mendicants and the "serious novel" became a commercially endangered species, science fiction survived as a literature supported entirely by the proceeds of sales to readers. If this has always been a two-edged sword, it has also always meant that a need for such a literature has always been felt by more than enough readers to support its existence.

Since I started writing the STAYIN' ALIVE column for *Locus,* of course, the publishing industry has gone well into the process of genrefying everything else the way it has always genrefied science fiction. At the same time, science fiction's market share was being pushed up by the grass roots. It became noticed. It became bigger business. It became enmeshed in the corporate decision-making process.

What will happen next? Well, for one thing, we're seeing the emergence of more than one sf genre. In other words, the total market has now become big enough to carve up into more finely tuned demographic slices.

On one level, a genrefied format designed to key into adolescent power fantasies marketed toward the demographic perception of the *Star Trek* or Star Wars generations.

On another level, science fiction as usual for what is perceived as the core audience by the industry even today—the science fiction subculture.

And on a third level, that feat of prestidigitation, the mainstream science fiction novel.

The what?

The mainstream science fiction novel. "Mainstream" now being defined entirely by the bottom line. Mainstream meaning an A book with A marketing and "genre" meaning a B book with B marketing. When *everything* becomes a genre, the only meaning genre distinctions have are the numbers. Just as I once defined science fiction as "anything published as science ficiton," so do industry parameters now define "mainstream" as anything published as an A book.

Riddley Walker, for example, was mainstream in boards, but won't make it as an A book in paperback. *Children of Dune* became a best seller without real A book treatment, a grass-roots effect. But *God Emperor of Dune,* even with its pulp title and hardcore sf content, was no surprise best seller; it was marketed as an A book and became a mainstream best seller according to expectations.

What is beginning to happen is that the publishing industry, in its usual laggardly fashion, is beginning to learn from the grass roots. Even though science fiction had been confined to a genre ghetto, and not without detrimental effects on the quality and seriousness of the literature itself, its inherent sphere of discourse was becoming more and more central to the problems of society, and the general public consciousness was inevitably developing a hunger for something like science fiction in its intellectual center. Even if it didn't know yet that something existed to feed it.

In other words, up until, say, *Star Wars,* there were many people who would have had an itch scratched by science fiction who barely understood what it was, to whom it was somehow inaccessible.

What made science fiction inaccessible to the general reading public? Well, of course, the sleazoid packaging didn't exactly attract an intellectually upscale audience, since they were not part of the demographic slice at whom the stuff was commercially targeted. Which in turn did not have a positive effect on the ambition of the writing. Of course, there was always a sophisticated audience of *some* size who recognized what was going on behind the packaging. And so, ambitious science fiction novels tended to be written for this perceived reader, someone who already knew the language and imagery.

This, in a way, encouraged some fine novels to be written, since they could, in effect, be written for people who knew as much as the writer. There is something to be said for the compaction achievable by use of a complex system of stylized imagery shared with the readership.

But of course, to those who don't speak the secret language, it's all about as accessible as the Mayan Codex.

The Space Program, *Star Trek,* and then *Star Wars* broke the secret code. When men were really going to the Moon with commentary by Walter Cronkite, all the space imagery of science fiction stopped being proof of crackpottery and started looking like prophecy. *Star Trek* in a way was a work of genius. For the first time, someone invented a science fiction genre format targeted at a mass audience. In its three years of lousy first-run ratings, an average of 20 million people saw each episode. Over the years, probably every man, woman, and child in the United States has become familiar with the Starship Enterprise, its Vulcan First Officer, and its somewhat paranoid crew. It has entered public folklore.

And it brought science fiction imagery with it.

It made all that space stuff accessible. And George Lucas cashed in big. You knew it from the moment he started the film with "Once upon a time in a galaxy far, far away...." He wasn't wasting any time establishing science fiction imagery for a supposedly uninitiated mass audience. There you were right in the middle of it before the first shot.

The publishing industry, being not nearly as capital-intensive as film-making and therefore not as paranoidly attuned to the Nielsens, has taken longer to realize that sf imagery is no longer inaccessible to a mass audience.

But you don't have to be a genius to finally realize that if a science fiction movie can be the biggest grosser of all time, there are more than enough demographics for a very large national best seller which does not require tens of millions of customers.

The fabulous Carl Sagan deal puts the seal on the mainstream sf A-book best seller. $2 million. $1 million in pre-sold foreign rights. A movie deal. All on an outline. Who can deny that this is the major leagues?

Now a lot of people grumble that Sagan could only make such a deal for an unwritten first novel because he was already a big-time celebrity with ready access to the creme de la creme of media PR.

And, of course, that's all true. But the point is that there's nothing very unusual about it. This is the way blockbuster best sellers come into being.

The point is that all this razzle-dazzle and moola is *not precluded* for a science fiction novel. A novel about first contact with intelligent aliens, yet.

So from here on in, we're going to have A science fiction novels and B science fiction novels. Just as every genre of the mainstream mosaic now has its A and B books.

Now in the nature of things, there's probably room for no more than half a dozen viable A mainstream sf novels a year. And by the nature of things, those who know how to do these deals or who have best-seller credits rather than genre credits are going to get the lion's share. At least until more science fiction writers receive a higher (and lower) education in how things really work in the marketplace. And even then, there still aren't that many chances to break the bank.

So, like most other fiction writers, science fiction writers are going to have to contend with genrefied publishing. It's a new game now. For one thing, the top end of genre sf is cut off.

During the 1970s Sf Boom, we saw some science fiction novels sell big within the genre. I think we're going to see less of that. As soon as publishers conceive of a science fiction novel as having mainstream demographics, they will pull it from the regular genre science fiction line with its genre packaging and package it as a mainstream science fiction novel to be marketed accordingly.

A genre logo on a science fiction novel will place a ceiling on its sales. A genre publishing program will ultimately lose the science fiction novels it would most like to publish, at least in terms of the bottom line. The books that should be leading its line will be published on other lists within the same house. A strong genre package becomes its own self-defined upper limit.

Paradoxically, though, there is the possibility of applying a variation of the overall strategy to survival at a high level *within* the genre. Because a mass audience for mainstream science fiction has come into being, it doesn't necessarily mean that the audience for genre sf has shrunk.

The cross-breeding of science fiction and fantasy has evolved a powerful genre formula with deep psychological attraction for a larger audience than ever before, particularly among adolescents trying to develop positive self-images in a society in deep crisis. Once again, George Lucas had it right. By marrying hardware to the mystical Force, he simulated the longed-for fusion of science and spirit, and in a manner which zeroed right in on the nation's frustrated adolescent power fantasies.

But what he created was not art; by his own insistence, it was "entertainment." *Star Wars* perfected and updated the old genre formula, fusing "science fiction" with "fantasy" to create the "sf" or "science fantasy" format. And the elements of the mythos were as ruthlessly arranged along marketing parameters as the Iron Dream that Hitler sold to Germany.

The adolescent ingenue in all of us who is the secret hero of history, who will finally stand revealed as the darling of destiny. Lots of literally faceless enemies to slay along the way, no more subject to our human sympathies than a Kraut or a Dink or a Slope. Wonderful battle scenes to stir the sanguinary libido. A villain of perfect blackness. Loyal nigger robots. And finally, in the Force, the triumph of the will of the hero over mass-energy reality itself.

Whether the specific imagery you plug in is the spaceships and aliens of space opera, the barbarians and wizards of sword and sorcery, or the dragons and deities of high fantasy, the functional elements of the genre formula are the same, which is why they can now all be published under the "sf" logo.

This, of course, is not fiction about how things really work, it is fiction about how our power fantasies work, or more unpleasantly, fiction designed to masturbate same.

And while it is getting us off on guiltless Disneyland violence and making us feel like godlike heroes, it is telling us that our own will can conquer the laws of science.

In the science fantasy version, this ultimate ego trip is cunningly concealed in the seamless blending of scientific and technological image-systems with Jungian and Freudian logic. Here magic and science are portrayed as exactly the same thing, which means that things work however the genre imperatives want them to work to fulfill the archetypal power fantasy.

This fits into certain hungers in a rather large audience like a key in a keyhole guarding a money bin. The rejection of what so many see as the spiritual sterility of the universe as we scientifically perceive it. The spreading adolescent alienation from troubled personal reality which is scorned as mundane and into a more colorful universe of role-playing games, electronic games, computer games, and mind-cult games. The struggle of the superior being we all know ourselves to be to take its rightful place of glory at the top of the world.

And, of course, an Osterized blend of science and magic, mirroring the blurring in the macroculture, as epitomized, for example, in the successful formula of *Omni*, where space activism is advocated cheek-by-jowl with UFOlogy, and the "spiritual sciences" are handled continuously with biochemistry and medicine.

What can I say? In ruthless, bottom-line, amoral terms, there is no better way to design "sf" to sell. This, ultimately, is what genrefication means—to science fiction and to any other literary mode. You find the buttons, and you push them in the proper sequence, and the targeted reader gets off, and you maximize profit, and the story that gets told has no moral that bears examining. Like a good professional, not a debutante, you don't give the trick what you think he needs, but what you know he wants.

Given decent demographics (which the sf genre has), you can sell a large volume of product by saturating a genre with a lot of interchangeable genre-tailored books, as witness the stunning success of Harlequin romances.

Of course, you do lose an option in the process. When your line is a brand name for literary Big Macs, you lose the ability to exploit the exceptional novel, the one that can make you as much money as a couple of months worth of business as usual. You've got to sell a lot of Chevies to add up to one Rolls-Royce.

It seems to me that if B-book sf genre publishing is going to continue to exist and even thrive, each house is going to have to decide which way to go as a conscious decision. You can't have it both ways.

If you adopt rigid genre format packaging a la Timescape Books, you find, as David Hartwell did, that you can't keep potential mainstream sf novels like *The Vampire Tapestry* and *Timescape* in your line. You can't keep them because you can't package them as what they are, namely science fiction novels accessible to the larger audience for mainstream sf. Both *Timescape* and *Vampire Tapestry* did better as middle-list mainstream paperbacks than they ever could have done as a genre-packaged Timescape line-leaders.

On the other hand, you really *can't* package a high volume of formula product on a book-by-book basis, since what you are selling is the genre format itself on a continuous basis, not any one episode.

Will it prove impossible for any genre sf line to maintain what in golden oldies was euphemstically called a "balanced list"? Balanced, that is, between editorial idealism and the bottom line, between novels of high literary and/or high sales ambition, and the bread and butter need to churn out X number of books a month.

When we look at publishing in general, the answer seems to be no. Few books published in any genre format break through the package into A seller status. The more rigid and segregated the format and package, the more impossible this becomes.

But science fiction is somewhat unique. Its unpackaged imagery can proclaim its identity loud enough. These days there can hardly be a subliterate person in the United States who doesn't know what a starfield or a rocket ship or a robot or a ringed planet means. You could package a line of books with covers consisting entirely of standard lettering over a full-color starfield and no one would mistake them for nurse novels.

You don't need a logo or a packaging style to identify a line of sf on the racks. You can use cartoon drawing, movie poster realism, astronomical photographs, NASA picture handouts, Daliesque surrealism, or any other visual style, and it doesn't matter because science fiction cover art identifies the product by imagery itself.

So you can hire one or two artists to do your regular B science fiction line in a consistent style, which is to say, their consistent painting style, period. And then you can simply use different artists to package your A science fiction novels in mainstream sf style using the same imagery. As long as the A and B books are not tied together by consistent packaging, you can do both to maximum effect in the same line, and also regain the flexibility to do justice to the vanishing middle-list book, the monthly leader.

As to how this all affects what is written and the people who write it, there is nothing new in the existence of a dialectic between art and commerce, of the conflict and interplay of artistic and economic imperatives, of moral ambiguities along the interface.

Formats sell. They sell because they were designed to sell and nothing else, with all the cunning and all the morality of the television commercials that spawned their present dominance.

Best sellers, A books, the mainstream mosaic of house-leading books have their own genre parameters by and large these days. For the most part, the A novels that best fulfill the A-novel formats of their genres will be the biggest hits, because they will be perceived so by their publishers and pushed accordingly.

In the microcosm as in the macrocosm. The best sellers *within* the genre sf universe will also tend to be those novels which best fulfill *their* genre format.

This is a fact of life in *any* genrefied literature. And it is also a fact of life that what makes big bucks for the corporation makes big bucks for the writer in the usual proportion.

Yet, since by the very nature of genre publishing there are a large number of what are considered interchangeable books published every month, written for low advances and not promoted, less attention is paid by the corporate decision-making process to what is really inside their interchangeable covers. It's still highly possible to get non-format sf published. It's also still possible to publish your taste.

The question facing all writers of fiction in the 1980s will be how to interface with the new realities of genrefied corporate publishing. Strategic decisions will have to be made, but also esthetic and moral ones, and they won't be easy.

A science fiction writer, given talent, will have three options: to attempt the mainstream science fiction novel, to fulfill the genre format, or to write what he wants to write for its own sake and then do what he can on the market.

In reality, of course, we will all be doing mixtures of all three, in the name of survival, art, or riches.

Publishers and particularly editors will face a similar decision every time they publish a list. In the best of all worlds according to writers, editors would always buy what is closest to their hearts and then cause the house to sell it like hotcakes. In the best of all worlds according to the corporate decision-making process, profit is maximized, period, and by the best available means.

In the real world, the way things work is that neither the ideal world of the writer nor the cold equations of the balance sheet can exist in isolation from each other. Any more than the things of the spirit can exist in isolation from the universe of mass and energy. Without some attention to the balance sheet, we have the present commercially non-viable avant-garde, all but invisible, and not *all* of it is empty pretension. Without some idealistic intent, the ratings go down after the first year or two, and the flop rate increases. At present the flop rate is over 50% in the publishing industry, a rate of failure which seems to be accepted as normal at a time when the industry is singing the blues.

If you address the dialectic of art and commerce from a science fictional viewpoint, the way things really work is that economic choices inevitably have artistic and social consequences, and esthetic and moral choices affect the bottom line. In a healthy society, this is an exquisitely balanced feedback relationship of satisfying ambiguity and complexity.

When the bottom line exercises overweaning domination, the corporate mechanism dominates art, and pressures it down toward the lowest common format denominators. First the literature devolves under negative evolutionary pressure, and then the flop rate soars (as in new TV formats) because the mechanism is not programmed to factor in abstracts like "quality." Which, however, sometimes does come home to roost on the balance sheet in its own sweet time nevertheless.

Should art absolute ever win a total victory over commerce to the point where a mode of fiction becomes entirely a dialogue among writers and critics in the absence of a demographically viable audience as reflected by sales, it's almost by definition out of business, as witness the plight of the "avant-garde."

When creative artists can maintain creative control of their own work and still make a living *within* something like economically viable parameters, when the artistic impulse and the overall bottom line can be balanced against each other by people rather than by homeostatic mechanisms, you can then at least have some kind of shotgun marriage of commerce and art in which both are forced to comprehend that there are times when both interests must be served.

This is a spirit that is fast disappearing from the world of fiction publishing. But it is a spirit which has not yet expired within what still remains a science fiction community. Ghetto survivors cannot help but have street smarts. And visionary dreamers can learn how to do business. And have been known to kick ass.

From a science fictional perspective, that's how things really work. The price of liberty is taking care of business, and the business of publishing needs human spirits at the helm. We still retain that, however uncertainly, in the sf realm. If we look unflinchingly at what's happening to writers in general, we may realize we still have a handhold on something precious worth preserving. Worth making certain economic compromises for.

But not at the expense of stayin' alive.

* * * * * *

(Shortly after the body of this book was typeset, events in the publishing industry bore out every one of Mr. Spinrad's predictions with the absorption of Fawcett and its subsidiaries by Ballentine/Del Rey, and the absorption of Ace/Charter/Grosset & Dunlap by Berkley (barely over its previous acquisition of Jove/Pyramid) and the purchase of Playboy by the same corporation. Appended below is a shortened version of Mr. Spinrad's column on this occasion.)

SEPTEMBER '82
COLUMN #21

Well, the other shoe has finally fallen; MCA-Putnam-Berkley-Jove has bought Grosset-Ace, absorbed Playboy Books as well, and the Reaganoid Justice Department has done exactly what one would have expected it to do, namely nothing.

Within the space of about half a year, sf publishing, not to say the publishing industry itself, has taken a quantum jump further toward conglomeratization. . . .

The first stage of this process was vertical, with the heavyweight entertainment conglomerates collecting publishers as subsidiaries. Now we are seeing the beginning of the horizontal phase, in which the likes of MCA and CBS and Orion and so forth trade publishing houses like baseball cards, and reshape the publishing industry itself almost accidentally in the process.

I say *almost* accidentally because now an overall pattern appears to be emerging out of all this random corporate fun and games.

A look at what these moves have done to sf publishing will give you a good idea of what the future of American publishing itself is going to look like down the pike; as so often before, sf writers and editors find themselves selected for the first wave to hit the beach. . . .

I say we may miss Ace Books more than we now realize. But of course we have been assured by the new management that Ace will continue to be published as a separate line.

Under the editorship of Susan Allison, who is also editing Berkley sf. Who is now, in theory, responsible for four Berkley and nine Ace titles a month. With a staff of "three or four people." If you still don't get the point, Victor Temkin spelled it out in words of one syllable in this very publication:

...more units with less overhead is the whole future of the business. We have seventeen salesmen on the road; they have ten. Between us, we should only have twenty or twenty-one, which saves us $300,000 a year. Editorial should have three or four people in science fiction, not three or four for each company. They have to read the same books. We'll need one or two more production people and one or two more in art, but not a whole staff.

True to his word, the entire Ace art department, its production people, and most of its editorial personnel were flushed down the tube when the deal was finalized.

What does this mean? What it means is classic horizontal conglomerate tactics, which, in another era, might be less euphemistically described as combination in restraint of trade. Certainly the effect is combination in restraint of trade and a severe shrinkage in editorial and publishing industry employment, bearing in mind that Ballantine is digesting Fawcett in a similar manner and Playboy Books has disappeared utterly.

Where are we now?

If we are editors, and we have thus far managed to hold on to our jobs, we are, like the man buried up to his neck in horse manure, in no position to make waves. Even when we are given additional work with inadequate staff without commensurate additional compensation. Because all we have to do is look at all the editors who are now out of work with little prospect in the drastically reduced job market to know how lucky we are to still have our heads above the surface....

Perhaps there are writers who do not find this tactic despicable. Perhaps there are some writers who do not feel that the welfare of editors is any of their business. Perhaps there are even some writers who believe that "increasing volume without increasing overhead" will work to their economic advantage.

After all, if there is less overhead charge for books, meaning a higher profit margin, that means more money to lavish on authors. Sure it does. And of course the same corporate thinking which in effect is already beginning to use the unemployment situation among editors (a situation quite deliberately created by publishing mergers) to cut editorial costs is going to turn around and share its ill-gotten gains with the authors.

You have, of course, noticed how the past year or two's corporate mergers have already redounded to the economic benefit of writers. You *haven't?* Instead, what you've seen is a few huge deals for a few blockbusters, and a downward pressure on respectable middle-level advances?

Well, look where we have arrived now. Dell is gone. Fawcett is vanished. Doubleday has cut its list in half. Playboy Books is dead. Del Rey is still trying to digest Fawcett SF, and Ballantine has a major case of the bends from swallowing a goat bigger than itself....

It's safe to say that at best Ace and Berkley will not be doing very much purchasing either, not unless the enormous Ace list is absorbed into some sensible schedule. That this will level off at anything like thirteen titles a month lacks a certain credibility. This would be twice what anyone else is now doing. Maybe Ace will survive as an imprint. Maybe Ace and Berkley will be able to do nine or ten books a month between them. But even under this optimistic scenario, we have still lost the equivalent of another major sf publisher, both in titles per month and in the sense of being another independent market. . . .

Rumors of stage terminal have already surfaced. Independent bookstores are folding. Partly as cause and partly as effect, publishers are refusing to extend credit to more and more of them. As a result, the massive bookstore chains like Dalton and Walden are gobbling up market share. Now comes the sinister intelligence that certain publishers are considering having executives from major bookstore chains sitting on their editorial boards.

From a corporate viewpoint, why not? The major book chains buy centrally. If present trends continue, they will utterly dominate the retail market within the decade. Who wouldn't want this retailing monolith telling you how many copies to print of what? Because they'd really be te will at last be fully integrated both vertically and horizontally. Everything will be totally in its control from point of purchase of point of sale.

Is this where we are heading? Maybe half a dozen big publishing combines with scores of imprints, each of them hooked up with a major book chain? Rack sales controlled as today by area monopolies but losing market share to the three-dimensionally conglomeratized giants? . . . .

If the corporate game of the future is less overhead per unit cost, that means fewer books published. If it isn't also to mean decreased receipts, it must also mean more copies sold of each book. Fewer products, fewer retail outlets, economies of scale, a permanent buyer's market for books, and more unit sales per production, just like Hollywood where, these days, anything that didn't gross $100 million is almost considered a bomb. . . .

Moreover, the turnover rate will more and more be in a complex feedback relationship with the *expectations* of the buyers for the chains. If you convince Walden and Dalton that a book will move, they will purchase it in quantities and display it in a manner that will make it move.

So, if you want to look for a silver lining in all these dark clouds, it could be that sf publishers are finally going to be *forced* to package each novel to count. It may very well be that *this* market contraction will end up falling most heavily on what is perceived as interchangeable product in the middle and the bottom of the lists. A lot of writers will get poorer, but those at the top will get richer.